The Author

Ramachandra Guha played cricket for St Stephen's College, Delhi, alongside two former captains of Indian Schoolboys and two future Test cricketers. He then went to Calcutta to do a doctorate, embraced Marxism, and gave away his collection of cricket books. Spurned by the Marxists, he returne'd to cricket, thereby reversing the path taken by the great British socialist H.M. Hyndman, who became a Marxist only after failing to win a Cricket Blue at Cambridge.

During the week Ramachandra Guha works in a leading social science research institute in Delhi. He is now rebuilding his cricket library.

Wickets in the East

An Anecdotal History

by

Ramachandra Guha

With Illustrations by M. A. Salam Khan

DELHI

OXFORD UNIVERSITY PRESS

BOMBAY ◆ CALCUTTA ◆ MADRAS

Oxford University Press, Walton Street, Oxford OX2 6DP
NEW YORK TORONTO
DELHI BOMBAY CALCUTTA MADRAS KARACHI
PETALING JAYA SINGAPORE HONG KONG TOKYO
NAIROBI DAR ES SALAAM
MELBOURNE AUCKLAND
and associates in
Berlin Ibadan

Printed at Crescent Printing Works Pvt Ltd., New Delhi 110001
and published by S. K. Mookerjee, Oxford University Press
YMCA Library Building, Jai Singh Road, New Delhi 110001

For three uncles : Durai, Shankar and Cheenu;
and two friends : Shivy and T.G.V.

Contents

There are no cricketers like those seen through twelve-year-old eyes.

Ian Peebles

Acknowledgements

The dedication to this book expresses a debt to my closest
cricketing colleagues. Among them, I must single out N.
Duraiswami, a left arm spinner of uncommon ability well
known in cricketing circles in Delhi and Bangalore for narrowly failing to play first class cricket, despite having only one
arm. A goodly number of the stories in this book, and certainly
the best ones, are from Durai. As for the rest, I have relied
heavily on 'native informants' from the different cities, states,
and city-states of Indian cricket. Among the more reliable of
these informants were : V. Chander; Partha Chatterjee; S.V.
Kumar; Raju Mukherji; Rudrangshu Mukherjee; and P.K.
Srinivasan. I have also drawn freely on memories of days spent
in the sun, but strictly beyond the boundary. And even a history
as outrageously informal as this one has to take note of the
printed word : my principal debts in that regard are indicated
at appropriate places in the text.

My wife, Sujata, saw this Luddite and his manuscript
safely in and out of the word processor. I was also fortunate in
having Sujit Mukherjee, author of four cricket books (with a
fifth, *Autobiography of an Unknown Cricketer*, in preparation),
stay but a sharp throw from cover point away from my own
wicket. Finally, I must thank Ashis Nandy, without whose

ix

provocation this book would not have been begun; and Rukun Advani, without whose encouragement it would never have been completed.

Honouring our Heroes

*M*y first cricketing heroes were, naturally, my father's. In 1940, as a boy of sixteen, he travelled halfway across the subcontinent to spend a holiday with his sister in Bombay. There he watched a day of the cricket season's grand finale, the match between the Ranji Trophy champions, Maharashtra, and a Rest of India side. Maharashtra were captained at the time by the Sanskrit professor, D.B. Deodhar. Deodhar had been judged too old, at forty, to be selected for the 1932 tour of England. Now, eight years older, he had just concluded his most successful season, highlighted by a remarkable quarter-final against the team most favoured to win the Ranji Trophy, Bombay. In that match, Deodhar had scored a flawless double century in his side's score of 675; then, with Bombay on the threshold of the crucial first innings lead at 600 for 5, he had claimed the third new ball to hustle out the remaining batsmen just short of Maharashtra's own total.

While he remembers Professor Deodhar well, my father's overall memories of the match are hazy, and with contemporary newspaper accounts not at hand I can only guess the names of some of the cricketers he watched that day at the Brabourne Stadium. The Maharashtra side must have relied

1

heavily on the all-rounder with the film star looks, S.W. 'Ranga' Sohoni, and the peerless Vijay Hazare, not yet capped for India but already a legend owing to his feats in the Bombay Pentangular. (The Pentangular, contested between Hindus, Muslims, Parsis, Europeans and The Rest, was at the time Indian cricket's premier tournament.) As for Rest of India, its fast bowler, with Amar Singh dead and Mohammed Nissar on the verge of retirement, would most likely have been Shute Bannerjee, its main spinner the youthful Vinoo Mankad—like Hazare yet to play in an official Test.

Of Sohoni and Hazare, Bannerjee and Mankad, my father has only the faintest recollections. His most vivid memories are of Deodhar's counterpart in the Rest of India side, Lala Amarnath. In that one day Amarnath batted, bowled, fielded, captained and, after an injury to his team's stumper, kept wickets as well. He was to do all these things on a more famous occasion, during the Bombay Test match against the West Indies in 1949.

Having demonstrated his skill in every aspect of the game, Lala was for my father the Complete Cricketer. While playing club cricket in Bangalore and Dehradun my father, especially when he was captain, tried to emulate the Lala by batting, bowling, fielding and then prevailing on his keeper to hand over the gloves.

Yet such occasions were infrequent. More often, my father was just an ordinary member of the team, and then his role model was not the Lala but his other boyhood hero, C. Ramaswami of Madras. Whereas he had journeyed a thousand miles to see Amarnath, he watched Ramaswami play in a tournament in the southern town where he grew up, Mangalore. A noted left-handed hitter, Ramaswami took his stance with the bat held well aloft, a stance since resurrected by Tony Greig, though solely for defensive purposes. Positioned thus,

Ramaswami dared the bowler to pitch up to him, and when he did, struck the ball for six after six. Although, unlike Ramaswami, my father batted right-handed, he adopted the hitter's flamboyant stance, and likewise founded his game on the lofted drive.

My father's choice of heroes may have been purely accidental, but, between them, Amarnath and Ramaswami frame the social history of Indian cricket in its formative phase, *circa* 1925 to 1950. Educated at Cambridge, where he took a degree in agriculture, Ramaswami was very much the sportsman of leisure; in fact, he turned to first class cricket only at the culmination of a no less distinguished tennis career (he won a Blue at Cambridge, and also played for India in the Davis Cup). At forty, he was the second oldest cricketer to be capped on debut for India. He came from a family of wealth and influence in Madras, which, among other things, endowed the city's most prestigious cricket tournament, named for Ramaswami's father, Buchi Babu Naidu.

By contrast, cricket for Amarnath was not a pastime but a vehicle for social advancement. Born two thousand miles to the north, in the small Punjab town of Kapurthala, he first made his mark as a wicket-keeper for the Aligarh University team. His precocious skills were brought to the notice of that early patron of Indian cricket, Maharaja Bhupendra Singh of Patiala, whose staff Amarnath then joined. Selected for India shortly after he had turned twenty, Amarnath made a brilliant hundred on his Test debut, against England at Bombay in 1933. But whereas Ramaswami, in the aristocratic fashion, could only bat, the Lala had to cultivate a variety of skills: starting out as a wicket-keeper batsman, he became in time the country's finest swing bowler. Lacking an independent source of income, Amarnath's cricket career stretched on; twenty years after his Test debut he was recalled to captain India in its first series against Pakistan. He played in the Ranji Trophy tournament for another decade, and made his living as a cricket coach until he was nearly seventy.

A more significant difference between my father's two boyhood heroes lies in their respective cricketing statures. Ramaswami was very much a 'local'—or more accurately, regional—hero, a man of the South, best known for his hitting in the annual Madras Presidency match between Indians and Europeans. It was the plebeian Amarnath who more fully represented the aspirations of a nation in the making. The settings in which my father saw them play underscores this contrast—whereas the Lala played at what was then the undisputed home of Indian cricket, Bombay's Brabourne Stadium, Ramaswami hit his sixes on the grounds of the Ganapathi High School, on the sea front at Mangalore. Indeed, Amarnath was captain in the first Test series played by India as an independent nation, against Australia in 1947. His opposing captain in that year was also always referred to by the definitive prefix— for Bradman was *the* Don, just as surely as Amarnath was *the* Lala.

However, India's captain in its last series as a colony— against England in 1946—was inevitably a prince, the senior Nawab of Pataudi. When the Australian tour came along, Vijay Merchant, an able representative of the Indian capitalist class which had financed the nationalist Congress Party, was first chosen to lead the team. After Merchant withdrew, a member of the lower middle classes which had sustained the national movement was named as his replacement. And when Amarnath retained his job for the first series independent India played at home, against the West Indies in 1948–9, the Indian Cricket Board was congratulated by the legendary Caribbean allrounder Learie Constantine. If India could appoint a commoner and not an aristocrat as captain simply because he was

4

the best man for the job, so, he felt, should the West Indies. Constantine's plea went unheeded—it was another decade and a half, and only after most Caribbean nations had won their own independence, that Frank Worrell was able to decisively challenge the prejudice that only educated whites could captain the West Indies.

II

Many of the cricketers described in this book strutted confidently, like the Lala himself, on the world's stage; others, like Ramaswami, were primarily provincial stars who barely made it into Test cricket; still others, for example B. Frank of Mysore and A.G. Ram Singh of Madras, are deservedly folk heroes in their own cities but never played for India. In what follows, I explore the local roots of Indian cricket, even as I establish the links between locality, province and nation. For international stars like Amarnath, my intention is to restore them to their original homes (homes to which most of them have since returned); simultaneously, I hope to bring what are primarily local heroes to wider notice.

In honouring our heroes, I use a device much favoured by bored schoolboys in classrooms—namely making up imaginary elevens. However, the practice of choosing elevens was recently resorted to, in his *History of West Indies Cricket*, by no less a person than the Prime Minister of Jamaica, Michael Manley. True to his profession, Manley did things in style. In a contest that would for once merit the copywriter's well-worn line, 'The Match of the Century', he picked two World XI's to play Mars, at home and away respectively.

The practice of making up hypothetical teams has served cricket lovers well in the long months—winter or summer, depending on one's hemispheric location—when the game

5

itself is in abeyance. Its origins are obscure. Perhaps it first started in England, in whose wet climate matches are punctuated by endless halts for bad weather, leaving spectators at a loose end. In any case, it has found favour in all cricket-playing countries, and seems especially suited to the leisurely pace of our own agrarian civilization. A means of affirming a continuing commitment to cricket, inside and outside the playing arena, it gives full rein to the endemic disease of cricket lovers—the playing of favourites. For reasons that cannot always be fathomed, we identify more with particular players and particular teams. It is impossible to resist this urge to favouritism: thus, Manley changed one of his World XI's at the last moment, dropping Walter Hammond and inserting the former West Indian captain, Viv Richards, in the proofs of his book.

Of course, our preferences are not always shared by the selectors. Our favourite players are never picked, and when they are, get dropped at the earliest opportunity. Making up our own elevens helps us get our backs on the selectors (so what if Y was dropped for the coming Test, he will be in *my* all-time Indian XI). But perhaps its most fascinating aspect is in its unexpected juxtapositions, as our imagination throws together players whose careers would never have overlapped. Making up elevens is a source of endless pleasure, as one's favourites are given pride of place; endless frustration, as other favourites cannot be squeezed into what are after all only eleven places; and endless dispute, if, as is most often the case, the teams are chosen in conjunction with a friend.

Most cricket lovers' horizons are rather more modest than Manley's, and in keeping with the patriotic fervour that is such a visible feature of the modern game, they like above all to choose various national elevens. Picking an all-time Indian XI, for example, quickly engenders the familiar feelings of delight,

6

frustration and dismay that are inescapable when one begins making up teams. To have Gavaskar and Merchant opening the innings—an easy choice—is the purist's dream, as is the sharing of the new ball by the Farrukhabad Express, Mohammed Nissar, and the modern master of swing and cut, Kapil Dev Nikhanj. But there are only eleven places (as against the nearly three hundred players who have represented India), and the frustrations begin to mount. For if Kapil Dev is picked on account of his superior batting, it can only be at the expense of Nissar's legendary bowling mate Amar Singh, of whom Wally Hammond said that 'he comes off the pitch like the crack of doom'. Even more distressing is the failure of the country's greatest slow bowler, Bishen Singh Bedi, to command a place. As the difference between them was the proverbial short head, and as Vinoo Mankad was also a formidable customer with the bat, the Sardar of Spin would be edged out, but barely, for the left-arm spinner's slot.

And what about the middle order? I cannot imagine an eleven without C.K. Nayudu, for so long the embodiment of the game in this country. And if C.K. is chosen, he must of course be captain and bat at the pivotal position of number three—the place in the order claimed as of right by other great batsman-captains such as Hammond, Bradman and Ian Chappell. But in choosing thus we must leave out Mohinder Amarnath, a man at least as courageous as C.K. himself. Likewise, for numbers four and five my instinctive choices would be the men that Gavaskar and Merchant, our openers, will forever be paired with—namely G.R. Viswanath and Vijay Hazare. Despite the charm of Vishy and Hazare (both on and off the field) their inclusion will not be taken lightly by partisans who favour Vijay Manjrekar—like his son Sanjay beautifully balanced in attack and defense—or who favour Dilip Vengsarkar and Polly Umrigar, two equally distinguished torchbearers of the Bombay tradition of batsmanship.

Depending on the strength of our attachments to tradition and history—most cricket lovers would favour contemporary players—and the particular reconciliation we effect between favouritism and objectivity, each of us will come up with our own all time Indian XI's. My selection reads : Gavaskar, Merchant, C.K. Nayudu (captain), Viswanath, Hazare, Mankad, Kapil Dev, Kirmani (wicket-keeper), Prasanna, Nissar and Chandrasekhar, with Eknath Solkar as twelfth man. In my more naive moments, I believe that this eleven meets the strictest standards of objectivity, but of course that is not the case. A critic for whom I have the highest respect, K.N. Prabhu of the *Times of India*, has recently come up with his all-time Indian XI, with as many as four different names from the ones I have offered. Here perhaps lie the perennial attractions of playing favourites; it is a game, like cricket itself, productive of the most fertile disagreements.

III

As my favourite writer on the game, A.A. Thomson, once wrote: 'cricket's frontiers follow the broad outlines of geography and then of history'. In this book I illustrate Thomson's maxim with folk histories of Indian cricket's six great regional teams— Bombay, Tamil Nadu, Karnataka, Hyderabad, Delhi and Bengal. The choice of these six was pretty straightforward. All these teams have won the national championship, the Ranji Trophy, in the past, and all continue to be strong contenders today. Indisputably the home of Indian cricket, for many years (1958 to 1974) the island city of Bombay had made the trophy its own. The three southern teams, Hyderabad, Karnataka (earlier Mysore) and Tamil Nadu (previously Madras), have been consistently among the best, and their rivalry for what was

8

earlier one and are now two places in the knock-out rounds of the Ranji Trophy has informed some of the most memorable matches in the competition. Under the inspirational leadership of Bishen Singh Bedi, Delhi and North Zone emerged to successfully challenge the hegemony of the South and West. Bengal is perhaps not as major a cricketing power as the other five, but it does have the most avid cricket followers. At any rate cricket, like all things of British origin—whether good, bad or indifferent—was introduced there well before it appeared in other parts of India. I must also confess here to a desire to undo the sense of neglect that Bengalis have historically felt with respect to the national mainstream, in which feeling the lack of recognition of Bengali cricketers has played no mean part. Indeed a Calcutta journalist recently described his city's relations with the rest of India as 'one long conspiracy against the Boses'. Significantly, his list of spurned Boses included, apart from the politicians Khudiram and Subhas and the scientist Jagadish Chandra, two fine batsmen who never played for India—Kartik and Gopal. But this journalist could just as easily have spoken of a Greater Indian Conspiracy against the Bannerjees—the nationalist Surendranath, the musician Nikhil, the actor Victor, and the fast bowlers Shute and Montu, who only played one Test apiece.

While six states merit individual treatment, the book ends with two composite chapters. In these I first take up Baroda and Rajasthan, two fragments of princely India which still have active teams in the Ranji Trophy. The next chapter pairs two great combinations of the past, Ranji's Nawanagar and C.K. Nayudu's Holkar, both winners of the Ranji Trophy in their time but doomed to disappear with the integration of princely states within the Indian Union.

At the risk of subverting the unity and integrity of the country by fostering regional chauvinism, I shall choose the all-time elevens of these ten states. Although in each case I end up with eleven names, the book's primary purpose is to evoke the folklore of the game and its practitioners. To that end, each chapter highlights trends and personalities that exemplify the cricketing culture of these different Ranji Trophy teams. Here, playing favourites is merely an excuse, albeit a delightful one, for exploring the highways and byways (or more accurately, the *gullies* and *mohallas*) of the cities and states of Indian cricket.

CHAPTER ONE

Jore Ball in Bengal

*T*he cricketing history of Bengal is lacklustre when compared to the star-studded narratives of Bombay, Delhi and Karnataka. Indeed, cynics may remark that Bengal's (and East Zone's) most significant contribution to Indian cricket was the failure of its representative to attend the crucial selection committee meeting of 1970. This representative was the versatile Datta Ray, whose achievements on the playing field are unrecorded, but who was also for a time national football selector. Datta Ray's absence, it may be recalled, enabled Vijay Merchant to give his casting vote in favour of Ajit Wadekar—and against the incumbent, Tiger Pataudi, whose claims Datta Ray would have supported—thereby inaugurating a new era in Indian cricket. But whatever the cynics may say, the oldest cricketing association and most literate cricketing public in the country surely have a more lasting claim on our attention.

For many years, and despite the recent challenges of Bihar and Orissa, Bengal has totally dominated East Zone cricket. However, until very recently this dominance was not translated into success at the national level. As for the representation of Bengal players in the national side, it has been subject to what can only be called, in a favourite phrase of Indian cricket

11

commentators, 'fluctuating fortunes'.

In the first phase, *circa* 1932–47, no Bengali played for India. Although the fast bowling all-rounder Shute Bannerjee made two tours of England, in 1936 and 1946, each time he returned without playing a Test. Indeed, after his name was announced in the playing eleven Shute was replaced by Baqa Jilani (a vastly inferior cricketer) for the Oval Test of 1936 only because Jilani had fulfilled his captain Vizzy's desire by abusing C.K. Nayudu at the breakfast table. Likewise, the opening batsman Kartik Bose could count himself distinctly unlucky never to be picked for an official Test. It is not inconceivable that in an age when British loyalists dominated Indian cricket, wider political allegiances influenced these omissions—and Bengal had been for decades the epicentre of the national movement. In the nineteen-thirties the Bengali sense of injustice was so acute that, at a dinner hosted by the Cricket Association of Bengal (CAB) on the eve of the Calcutta 'Test' against Lord Tennyson's team in 1938, the CAB President, R.B. Lagden, publicly complained of the neglect of Bengal players by the Indian selectors, a refrain picked up and amplified by the Calcutta press.

With Indian independence, Bengal's luck seemed to have turned. In the next decade the state contributed at least three cricketers who distinguished themselves at the highest level: P. (Khokon) Sen, that fine wicket-keeper who had an outstanding tour when all was crumbling around him in Australia in 1947; Pankaj Roy, whose several Test centuries and record opening stand with Vinoo Mankad more than made up for a string of zeros; and Dattatreya Gajanan Phadkar, the Bombay exile who was India's finest fast bowling all-rounder before Kapil Dev. Three Bengali seam bowlers—Shute Bannerjee (at last), Montu Bannerjee and Nirode Ranjan Chowdhury also played for India during this period.

This efflorescence was followed by a relative drought, *circa* 1960–75, when talented Bengali players either made international tours without playing Tests (Gopal Bose, Rusi Jeejebhoy) or, when they were picked for India, rarely lasted beyond a few matches (Ambar Roy, Subroto Guha). Now the Eden Gardens crowd sublimated their regional feelings by rooting for the two great *jamai babus* (sons-in-law) of Bengal cricket, Tiger Pataudi and Erapalli Prasanna. The two *jamai babus* didn't disappoint them either. Calcutta was the scene of some of Prasanna's greatest spinning triumphs—against England in 1972–3, against the West Indies two winters later—while Pataudi at least twice broke a prolonged run famine at the Gardens—against New Zealand 1964–5, against the West Indies in 1974–5. In the final phase, *circa* 1975 to the present, Bengalis have not had much better luck, and it is noteworthy that the state's two representatives in the national side during this period, Dilip Doshi and Arun Lal, have been immigrants and not sons of the soil.

I may be wrong, but there does seem to be a significant overlap between Bengal's cricketing and political fortunes. The first stage (of Shute Bannerjee and Kartik Bose) closely corresponds to the diminishing influence of Bengal over the freedom struggle, following Gandhi's capture of the movement's leadership from the noted Calcutta lawyer C.R. Das 'Deshbandhu'. This phase culminates in the scandalous removal in 1939 of Subhas Bose, the darling of Bengal, from the presidentship of the Congress Party. The second stage, of Roy, Phadkar and Sen, signals a major recovery, politically speaking, when the state's Chief Minister, B.C. Roy, was the uncrowned king of Bengal and a particular friend and favourite of the Prime Minister, Jawaharlal Nehru (the CAB itself was presided over at the time by the veteran Congressman Tushar Kanti Ghosh). The third and fourth stages, of course, overlap with the growing separation of Bengal from the national mainstream, as embodied in the eclipse of the Congress as a political force in the state. Here indeed is a fit topic for a Ph.D. thesis in political science: would the communist-dominated Left Front have ever come to power if the Indian cricket selectors had not so cruelly treated Ambar Roy, Subroto Guha, Gopal Bose, D.S. Mukherjee and Dipankar Sarkar? This is indeed a dissertation topic that even lends itself to post-doctoral research—for would the Left Front have stayed in power so long if Robin Mukherjee, Barun Barman, Amitava Roy and Sambaran Bannerjee had got their just deserts?

II

Lenin might have concluded from the history of modern Bengal that just as imperialism is the highest stage of capital-ism, communism is the highest stage of cricket chauvinism. The feeling of neglect is, in fact, a recurring theme in the folklore of Bengal cricket. There is little doubt that Shute Bannerjee was cruelly treated, but Bengalis insist that he was only the first of their cricketers to be handled in this manner. Take the case of N.R. (Putu) Chowdhury, who gave Frank Worrell no end of trouble in representative matches, yet played only two official Tests. In one of these, at Madras against the West Indies, Putu ran out Everton Weekes at 90, thereby breaking the great man's amazing run of six successive Test hundreds. Yet his dominance of one 'W' in the field impressed the selectors as little as did his dominance of the other 'W' with the ball.

In the folklore of the Maidan, that green expanse in central Calcutta where all good cricket is played, Bengal batsmen were even more unlucky. In one story, a leading Bengal batsman of the nineteen-sixties was told by a national selector on the eve of a Duleep Trophy final not to risk injury as he was in the party to England. Taking the man at his word, he withdrew from the match, only to find that this 'unfitness' was used against him in the selection committee to drop him from the England tour. Another gifted opening batsman made a century against Sri Lanka for India, but never played an official Test because—or so the Maidan follower would have you believe—Gavaskar said he was a poor runner between the wickets and would run him out. A third case, at once tragic and comic, concerns a former captain of Indian Schoolboys. On the verge of Test selection, he was smitten by a lovely Bengali film actress. When the lady spurned his advances, and then shifted to Bombay to pursue a career in Hindi films, the poor fellow cracked up and even lost his place in the Bengal team.

A very Bengali story, even as the feeling of being done against by Bombay and Delhi is a very Bengali sentiment (the latter dates at least to 1911, in which year India's capital shifted from Calcutta to Delhi). Learning painfully to live with such neglect, the Maidan and Eden Gardens crowds compensated in at least three ways. First, to borrow a favourite phrase of sociologists, they 'domesticated the exotic'. So Pataudi and Prasanna, both of whom married Bengali girls, were as privileged sons-in-law treated on par with sons of the soil. In fact, such domestication had a long history, for in the inter-War period Bengal cricket was itself dominated by outsiders, with no less than six Europeans playing in the first state team to have won the Ranji Trophy, in 1938–9. The two towering figures in this European phase of Bengal cricket were the all-rounder T.C. Longfield, a Cambridge Blue and in time the father-in-law of Ted Dexter, and the wicket-keeper batsman A.L. Hosie, of Hampshire. In the Maidan, Alec Hosie was known only as Amrit Lal, and Tom Longfield as Tulsi Chand, while the venerable R.B. Lagden, President of the CAB and a Cambridge Blue of an earlier generation, was christened Rash Behari.

Second, the few international successes enjoyed by Bengal players were quickly transferred from history into myth. Thus every Calcutta boy is told the story of how P. Sen warned Bradman he was going to stump him off Vinoo Mankad, which he inevitably did. Unable to find evidence of this in the Test scoreboards of the 1947 Australian tour, I assumed that the Bengalis had confused Mankad's famous warning, duly executed, to Bill Brown for backing up too far (an incident immortalized in the term 'mankaded,' still in vogue in Australia) with an alleged warning by Sen to Bradman. Then I came across a book by a Bengali writer whose picture captions repeated this legend—thus Ghulam Ahmed was described as 'India's only bowler captain' (this was 1957), Subhas Gupte as the 'diminutive storehouse of wiles', but the Bengal stumper simply as 'P. Sen, who stumped Bradman'.* This urged me to look again, and I finally found that Sen had indeed stumped Bradman off Mankad, not in a Test but in the match against South Australia. Even so, Sen would not have dared to warn the Don, but, as a case of David slaying Goliath, this gloss on history may be forgiven. (Of far greater importance to Indian cricket were the *five* stumpings Sen effected off Mankad in India's first ever Test victory, against England at Madras in February 1952.)

Third, in international matches the Eden Gardens suppresses its regional pride in favour of more inclusive loyalties— to India, and to the game of cricket itself. Calcutta crowds have had little time for big hitters or classical batsmen, being inclined more towards elegant strokeplayers like Worrell,

---

* ARBI (R. Bhattacharya), *Indian Cricket Cavalcade* (Eastlight Bookhouse, 1957), opposite page 181.

Harvey, Mushtaq Ali and Viswanath. A particular favourite was Vijay Hazare, and they were even willing to forgive Vijay for keeping his strokes under wraps on the many occasions he had to save the match for India. Playing a long defensive innings against one of the Commonwealth sides, Hazare suddenly launched into an extravagant extra-cover drive off George Tribe. An anguished cry came from the East Stand: 'Hazare, steady!'

III

Even the Indian selectors could not stop the Roys of Bengal from sending three representatives to the Test side, a record equalled by only one other family, the Amarnaths. The first Roy, Pankaj, was also the greatest. Pankaj, who played for much of his career wearing spectacles, batted at number eleven in his first representative match, for Combined Universities against the West Indies in 1948–9, but became in time India's foremost opening batsman. Best known for his world-record opening stand with Mankad, Roy had a fine run against the West Indies, and also scored a vital hundred in that 1952 Madras Test against England.

Although Pankaj's son Pronab, who played two Tests against England in 1982, was cast in the same careful mould, his nephew Ambar was a dazzler, an attacking left-hander who hit an explosive 48 with ten fours in his first Test innings, against New Zealand in 1969. In the late sixties and early seventies, Ambar had to vie with Sardesai, Jaisimha, Hanumant Singh, Durrani, Ashok Mankad and Wadekar for one of the places in the Test team open to competition. (Gavaskar, Viswanath and Pataudi, as and when they played, were automatic choices.) Ambar was born a decade too soon, for he would have been in his element in the one-day game. He first came to prominence when he led Calcutta University to its only Rohinton Baria victory, with centuries in both the semi-final and the final. (Two other members of that side were Dilip Doshi and Gopal Bose.) Ambar was a masterly player of spin; although he played from the crease, he played very late and cut savagely. In an innings of 150-odd against Karnataka in the mid-seventies, he established a mastery over Prasanna and Chandrasekhar worthy of those other left-handers, Wadekar and Milkha Singh.

All the Roys retain a warm place in the affections of their townsmen, and none more so than Pankaj. On the evidence of the only time I saw him play, however, Pankajda exemplified the bad luck that had dogged Bengal cricket. This was the veterans match organized on the occasion of the Golden Jubilee of the Cricket Association of Bengal, an institution that Roy himself—as player, captain, selector, coach and adminis-trator—had done more than anyone else to build. In this match Pankajda came in first wicket down, after the crowd had been spoiled by a dazzling exhibition of footwork by the seventy-year-old Mushtaq Ali, who cut and hooked Freddie Trueman as if it were Old Trafford in 1936. As for Roy himself, it was one of those days when he just could not get the ball off the square. Meanwhile, Mushtaq had given way to the sixty-year-old Vijay Hazare—like Mushtaq much loved by the Eden Gardens crowd—who proceeded to repeatedly drive Lance Gibbs through extra cover: a hard act to follow, and an even harder act to play alongside. Poor Pankajda did the only sensible thing and ran himself out.

An honoured guest at that CAB jubilee was Fred Trueman. A wag naughtily remarked that when the Yorkshire fast bowler was introduced to the Indians, he shook hands with all except Pankaj, whom he embraced. This was an insider's allusion to the fact that Trueman dismissed Roy for four zeros in Freddie's first Test series, in England in 1952. Pankaj failed to score five times in that series, the beginnings of what Sujit Mukherjee was to call his 'ample duckyard'.

Over the years Roy did acquire a reputation for being weak against fast bowling, but nothing became the man more than the manner in which he finally disposed of this myth. Several years after the opener had left Test cricket, Bengal played Hyderabad in a Ranji Trophy quarter-final. Hyderabad's spearhead was the fearsome Roy Gilchrist—one of the four West Indian fast bowlers called in that year by the Cricket Board, after India had lost a Test series five-zero in the Caribbean—to help overcome what was believed to be a national failing to come to terms with pace.

Still smarting from an early exit from the West Indies Test side (he was sent home from the 1958–9 Indian tour for insubordination after bowling beamers at his captain Gerry Alexander's former Cambridge teammate Swaranjit Singh of North Zone, and never played Test cricket again), Gilchrist had already relayed a message to Calcutta asking the Bengal boys to watch out. On the morning of the match, the Jamaican terror walked into the clubhouse of the Eden Gardens pavilion and ominously started bouncing a new ball on the floor. Roy was as unnerved as the rest of his team, and put himself down to bat at number four. At this there was a minor revolt in the Bengal dressing room, with the youngsters chiding Pankajda for failing to set an example. To his lasting credit, Roy changed his mind and went out to open. He scored two remarkable hundreds in the match, being especially severe on the West Indian. After he had hooked Gilchrist for three successive boundaries, the fast bowler gave up in disgust—finishing the over underarm, he walked off the field.

IV

The Roys were, of course, all batsmen. Scanning the history of Bengal cricket, one is struck by the absence of quality spinners. The only two Bengali slow bowlers of any note were the leg-spinners Soumen Kundu and Dipankar Sarkar. Sarkar had a magical tour of England with the Indian Schoolboys in 1967, before his powers of flight and spin suddenly left him, just as they were to leave Laxman Sivaramakrishnan twenty years later.

However, the three best spinners to play for the state were all immigrants. Two were off-spinners, Prakash Bhandari and S.K. Girdhari. Girdhari, who could make the ball hum like a top, came from Karachi and started his cricketing career in the Sind Pentangular. While other Hindu cricketers from that city moved down the west coast after Partition—G.S. Ramchand to Bombay, G. Kishenchand to Baroda—he travelled across the subcontinent to make his home in Calcutta. In time Girdhari moved even further east, ending his first-class career with the Assam Ranji Trophy team.

The greatest spinner to have played for Bengal also came from the west coast, from the town of Rajkot. There were at least four reasons why Dilip Rasiklal Doshi did not play earlier for India. These were: Bedi, Chandrasekhar, Prasanna and Venkataraghavan. In patiently waiting for Bedi to lose his powers, Doshi had the advantage of being a few years younger than his fellow left-arm spinners Padmakar Shivalkar and Rajinder Goel. Even so, his entry into Test cricket was the result of a chance remark by that great friend of Indian cricket, Rohan Kanhai. At a party at the conclusion of the 1979 England tour, when the waning skills of Bedi and Chandrasekhar had been so cruelly exposed, Kanhai advised the manager that an experienced hand like Doshi, rather than

20

a raw recruit, would be the most appropriate replacement for the Sardar. Gavaskar, who adored Kanhai (he named his son after him), happened to be listening, and one of his first acts on being appointed captain was to send for Doshi.

Doshi probably reckoned that Gavaskar's recommendation was no more than his due, for it was he who had introduced the Little Master to his future wife. At any rate, the bespectacled and studious Gujarati made the best of a brief Test career. After taking six wickets in his first Test innings, he reached one hundred wickets in next to no time (just over two years, as I recall), becoming the only player, apart from the illustrious Clarrie Grimmett, to make his Test debut and claim a hundred victims after he turned thirty. As a bowler pure and simple, Doshi was a throwback to an earlier era. He was a hopeless bat—Imran always reckoned on bowling him first ball—and an even worse field. He was invariably placed by his captain at mid-on, the fielding position Sir Robert Menzies once called 'the last refuge of mankind'. Yet, in this strangest of games, it was Doshi who ran out the fleet-footed Asif Iqbal in the latter's last Test innings.

Sadly, Doshi's considerable attacking skills were not always evident in Test cricket. More often, he put into practice the craft he learnt at the behest of Gavaskar: bowling six minute maiden overs off a three-step run. To watch Doshi bowl in one of Gavaskar's many defensive moods as captain was to see an Oscar-level performance—after every ball the deliberate resetting of the field to an inch, the slow wiping of glasses, the readjustment of a headband, and more than one false start.

V

In contrast to the paucity of spin, there has been a stunning array of fine seam bowlers from the state. Indeed, one might say that new ball bowling is the tradition of Bengal cricket. The founding figure in this long, unbroken tradition was Sarabindu Nath 'Shute' Bannerjee. Although he also played for Nawanagar, achieved prominence bowling for the Hindus in the Pentangular, and eventually made his home in Bihar, Shute was born in Calcutta, played for its university and made his Ranji Trophy debut for Bengal. Shute's mantle was passed on to Kamal Bhattacharjee, the inswing bowler who led the attack in the Bengal team of Tarak Chand Longfield and Amrit Lal Hosie.

When Shute played his only Test at the age of thirty-eight, he was the captain of Bihar. Two younger Bengal seamers also played one Test apiece in that series against the West Indies in 1948–9. S. (Montu) Bannerjee had a lively opening spell at the Eden Gardens, bowling Atkinson and having Rae l.b.w., but was then surprisingly dropped, while Putu Chowdhury had little success with the ball at Madras. Like Dattu Phadkar, Putu was later sent to Alf Gover's coaching clinic in London. It is entirely in keeping with the Bengal tradition of fast bowling that while Phadkar cut down his pace thereafter and concentrated on swing, Putu went to Gover bowling medium pace off-cutters and returned as a tearaway fast bowler.

In the next two decades—and despite Dr B.C. Roy—no Bengal seam bowler played for India, but several came close. There was Premangshu Chatterjee, the left-arm Killer of Jorhat—he took 10 for 20 there against Assam—who in the Ranji campaign of 1955–6 took fifteen wickets in the semi-final against Madhya Pradesh and seven wickets in the first innings of the final against Bombay. Two other Bengal new-ball bowlers considered Test prospects at the time were D.S. Mukherjee and Ramesh Bhatia (Vijay Merchant even compared the latter to Amar Singh). More recently, Barun Barman and Amitava Ray came briefly into prominence after each had dismissed the great Gavaskar in an Irani Trophy match, while Samar Chakravarthy and Subroto Porel at least deserve an honourable mention.

Towering above them all was Subroto Guha, like Shute Bannerjee a master of swing. Eighteen years after Bannerjee had bowled East Zone to a famous win over the West Indies on their first tour of India, Subroto took eleven wickets on the mat for a combined East and Central Zone side in the only defeat suffered by the West Indies on their 1966–7 tour. And in a manner reminiscent of Shute's own treatment at the Oval in 1936, Guha was named in the playing eleven for the Bombay Test against Australia in 1969, only to be dropped for the off-spinner Venkataraghavan, on the morning of the match. Contemporary with the famous spin quartet, Guha got very little bowling in his four Tests, but on one memorable occasion at Ferozeshah Kotla he knocked the unbowlable Bill Lawry's off stump out of the ground. I remember seeing the photograph of this truly astonishing feat in the next morning's newspaper. Perhaps Kapil Dev saw that picture too!

When other states of Indian cricket have, without exception, been partial to spin, how does one explain the persistence of this tradition of seam bowling in Bengal? For one thing, most cricketers in Calcutta start playing on the streets with a tennis ball, known locally as the 'Cambiz' (Cambridge) ball. It is almost impossible to spin the Cambiz ball with any control; moreover, as it is normally dipped in water, it fairly fizzes off the street. When Bengalis graduate to using the red cherry (known here as the 'deuce' ball) on the Maidan, two climatic factors continue to favour seam bowling: dew on the wicket owing to the nine o'clock start occasioned by the early sunset in this eastern city; and the breeze blowing in from the Hooghly River which runs along the western edge of the Maidan. Eden Gardens itself is just off the Hooghly, on the

23

Maidan's north-western corner, and indeed the swing bowler
Roger Binny, who had a fine record at the Gardens, is believed
to have been picked for the 1987 World Cup only because the
final (which India never reached) was to be played there.

These 'environmental' factors were given a further fillip
by the ready availability of role models. The Maidan's first
bowling heroes were the swing bowlers Shute Bannerjee and
T.C. Longfield. Then again, Dattu Phadkar played several
seasons for the state, while the Bombay and India fast bowler
Ramakant Desai invariably bowled with fire at the Gardens.
Moreover, several leading coaches were themselves seam
bowlers; pre-eminently Kamal Bhattacharjee, but also the
Surrey and England bowler, Bill Hitch, invited by the Maharaja
of Cooch Behar to coach on the Maidan in the nineteen-
thirties.*

I suspect, however, that one must additionally invoke a
deeper historical reason to account for the Bengali predilec-
tion for fast bowling. Like bomb throwing and body building,
new ball bowling must be viewed as part of a wider Bengali
response to the relentless British attack on an alleged physical
deficiency. 'The physical organization of the Bengali is feeble
even to effeminacy', wrote Macaulay in 1843, a prejudice
echoed half a century later by Lord Curzon's private secretary
Frank Dunlop Smith, who claimed that the Bengali had 'the
intellect of a Greek and the grit of a rabbit'.

* The Maharaja of Cooch Behar was a great patron of cricket in the city. Eden
Gardens had once belonged to his family, while in the inter-War period he hosted
many matches in his Woodlands ground in south Calcutta. I once innocently asked
a Bengali friend whether 'Cooch' could play too. 'Of course', came the indignant
reply, 'he was captain of Harrow.' A rejoinder pregnant with meaning; while it
reflects the continuing Bengali obsession with British values, there is also a barely
veiled allusion to that other Harrovian and pet aversion of the Calcutta
intellegentsia, Jawaharlal Nehru, a man whose feats on the cricket field are
unknown to posterity.

A magnificient exception to the Great Bengal Tradition of seam bowling—from Rajkot!

This cultural chauvinism inspired the official declaration of Bengalis as a non-martial race in the mid-nineteenth century. Since then, as the historian John Rosselli once noted, the Bengali elite has had a 'markedly physical sense of collective degradation'. This colonial stereotype was thoroughly internalized by the Bengalis, who then strenuously sought to overcome it through the pursuit of physical culture. Thus the intellectual giant of the Bengali Renaissance, Bankim Chandra Chatterjee—of whom Henry Ford might have said 'All History is Bankim'—had himself called for the development of *bahubol* or physical strength as the key ingredient for Indian nationalism. Taking Bankim's plea to heart, some Bengalis initiated the *akhara* (gymnasium) movement which, in time, threw up India's only Mr Universe (Monotosh Roy in 1952), while on the cricket field *bahubol* was transformed into *jore* (fast) ball.

And so, when the greatest of modern fast bowlers, Malcolm Marshall, called his autobiography 'Marshall Arts', it was a pun the Bengalis readily appreciated. Fast bowling has indeed been Bengal's martial tradition. Unfortunately, corporate sponsors are not known for their sense of history, and the MRF Pace Foundation came to be pitched in Madras rather than in Calcutta.

VII

Some critics may argue that such theorizing is beside the point, for in the history of Bengal spin is to seam as cricket is to football. One Bengali writer, Mihir Bose, even made the faintly absurd suggestion that if Bengal had retained control over the national movement, football rather than cricket would have become India's favourite game.

An emphatic repudiation of Mihir Bose's claim is to be found in the number of footballing cricketers. Pankaj Roy himself played at inside-right for the First Division side Sporting Union, and was good enough to represent the Indian Football Association against Burma in 1949. (Roy's uncle, T.K. Roy, helped found one of India's two greatest football clubs, East Bengal.) Nirmal Chatterjee, perhaps a finer strokeplayer than Pankajda, played many years as a thrusting forward for the club with whose name East Bengal's is indissolubly linked, Mohun Bagan. S.C. (Kanu) Deb also played football for Mohun Bagan and cricket for Bengal, while Robi Das played football for East Bengal and for Bengal in the Ranji Trophy, and was besides a member of the Indian hockey team.

The finest footballing cricketer was actually a cricketing footballer, Chuni Goswami of Mohun Bagan. In the Ranji Trophy final of 1968–9 he scored 96 and 84 for the losing side. Three years later Chuni, who had led India to a famous victory in the Asian Games soccer championship in 1962, led Bengal to honourable defeat in yet another Ranji final. Facing the might of Bombay, how Chuni must have wished that he had on his side the cricketing equivalents of Jarnail Singh and Simon Sunderraj, the undoubted stars of India's greatest ever football team.

VIII

In picking an all-time Bengal eleven, one must enforce a ban against the professionals—Baloo Gupte, Vinoo Mankad, Vijay Manjrekar, C.S. Nayudu, etc.—who played the odd season for the state. I have also reserved Dattu Phadkar, who stayed a while longer, for his home state of Bombay. In the event, nine native Bengalis will be joined by two domiciled ones, namely Doshi, as well as one of three Delhi batsmen who made their cricketing home (having all joined Calcutta's tea industry) in the state—Ashok Gandotra, Michael Dalvi and Arun Lal—all

brilliant fielders to boot. 'Piggy' Lal probably gets first prefer-
ence, on account of his stupendously long innings in the Ranji
and Duleep trophies. We then have:

1. Kartik Bose
2. Pankaj Roy (captain)
3. Ambar Roy
4. Arun Lal
5. Gopal Bose
6. Shute Bannerjee
7. P. Sen (wicket-keeper)
8. S.K. Girdhari
9. Kamal Bhattacharjee
10. Subroto Guha
11. Dilip Doshi

Manager and Patron: Maharaja of Cooch Behar

If this side is playing at home, in the Gardens, Girdhari
can make way for a seam bowling all-rounder like Chuni
Goswami.

A final word for the followers on the Maidan who are
patiently waiting for Calcutta cricketers to make it to the
national side. If history is any guide, their luck has begun to
turn. For Bengal, by winning the 1989–90 championship, have
ended a run of eight successive losing appearances in the final
of the Ranji Trophy. In this, their second successful Ranji
campaign, they were guided by four players of impeccable
bhadralok credentials—Ashok Malhotra, Rajeev Seth, Raja
Venkat, and Arun Lal. The last named is, of course, the most
loved Bengali cricketer since Tiger Pataudi, and 35,000 crowded
into the Gardens to cheer his match-winning innings in the
1989–90 final with shouts of 'Lal Salaam! Lal Salaam!'—a
punning salutation particularly appropriate to Bengal, for

'Lal' also means red, and the crowd were simultaneously saluting Arun's batsmanship and their favourite Red Flag. Strikingly, this resurgence of Bengal cricket has coincided with the reintegration of Bengal within the national mainstream. For the defeat of the Congress party in the general elections of 1989 brought to power a Prime Minister, V.P. Singh, for whom Bengal's own Communist Chief Minister, Jyoti Basu, is something of a father confessor. No doubt the Gangulys and the Mukherjees will soon walk cheek by jowl with the Manjrekars and the Tendulkars in the Indian Test team.*

* I wrote too soon. As this book goes to press, V.P. Singh's government has fallen, thus ending any hopes of adequate Bengali representation in the Indian cricket team.

CHAPTER TWO

Bombay : India's Yorkshire?

 f Yorkshire has been the cradle of English cricket,
Bombay has played an identical role in India.
The dominance of the two teams in their countries' cricketing histories is such that what is said
of Yorkshire—that if it is strong, England is strong—could just
as easily be said of Bombay and India. The similarities do not
end here. Both sides have specialized in classically correct
opening batsmen: for example, Sutcliffe, Hutton and Boycott
for Yorkshire; Merchant, Madhav Apte and Gavaskar for
Bombay. Again, both teams have been able to call upon, almost
at will, a succession of wily slow left-arm bowlers: Peel, Rhodes,
Verity and Wardle in the one case, Jamshedji, Mankad, Nadkarni
and Shivalkar in the other.

For the national side, Bombay players, like their counterparts in Yorkshire, have been—to use A.A. Thomson's phrase—
'hereditary breach stoppers'. When Sanjay Manjrekar and
Sachin Tendulkar guided India to four draws against an
infinitely superior Pakistan side in the winter of 1989, they
were carrying on a remarkable tradition initiated by Vijay
Merchant in the nineteen-thirties and forties, consolidated by
Vijay Manjrekar and Polly Umrigar in the fifties and sixties, and
raised to soaring heights by Dilip Sardesai, Sunil Gavaskar and

Dilip Vengsarkar in the seventies and eighties. The essential continuity of this tradition was brought home to me as I watched Sachin Tendulkar and Ravi Shastri bat at a particularly difficult phase of the Third Test. Young Sachin understandably wanted to hit his way out of trouble, and to temper his exuberance Shastri talked to him at the end of every over, his arm placed affectionately across the boy's shoulders. The sight of the giant Shastri and the tiny Tendulkar was a most affecting one, bringing to mind the guidance given to Gavaskar at a similar stage of his career by Dilip Sardesai, and in time to Vengsarkar by Gavaskar himself.

Bombay's great strengths, like Yorkshire's too, may be gauged by the number and quality of its cricketers who have gone to play for other states. Indeed, a team of Bombay exiles would be as formidable as the all-time elevens of most other states. A likely eleven, all of whom were Test cricketers, could read: 1. V. Mankad (Rajasthan—captain) 2. K.M. Rangnekar (Holkar) 3. V.L. Manjrekar (Rajasthan, Bengal, Uttar Pradesh and Maharashtra) 4. G.S. Ramchand (Rajasthan) 5. Ramnath Kenny (Bengal) 6. Sandeep Patil (Madhya Pradesh) 7. D.G. Phadkar (Bengal) 8. F.M. Engineer (Lancashire—wicketkeeper) 9. G.R. Sunderam (Rajasthan) 10. Subhas Gupte (Rajasthan) 11. Baloo Gupte (Bengal and Railways).

II

As a cricketing city, Bombay reflects its social geography, though perhaps not so strikingly as Hyderabad (see Chapter IV). In other words, within its city limits one may distinguish between two different kinds of cricketers, emerging from two distinct social milieux. Admittedly in Bombay, unlike Hyderabad, class distinctions do not always get reflected in cricketing styles, as witness the similar batting techniques of

31

that scion of an industrial empire, Vijay Merchant, and the quintessentially middle class boy made good, Sunil Gavaskar. It is, however, indisputable that one source of Bombay's cricketing wealth has been the Parsi and Gujarati elite, the two communities which, figuratively speaking, sit on top of Bombay society at Pali, Cumballa and Malabar hills. The Parsis, of course, were making their fortunes in the China opium trade even as they were taking to a game which more than one economist has since referred to as the opium of the people. The names of great Parsi cricketers are legion, and half a dozen of the best were the batsmen Rusi Modi, Polly Umrigar and Nari Contractor; the all-rounders P.E. Palia and Rusi Surti; and that jack-in-the-box behind the stumps, Farokh Manekji Engineer. Fine Gujarati players who have appeared for Bombay include Merchant, his batting mentor L.P. Jai, and the seam bowler Ramesh Divecha. On the other hand, by far the most stable source of talent especially since the nineteen-fifties, has been the solid Maharashtrian middle class localities of Dadar and Shivaji Park. And with the slow decline of the Parsi community and the transition in Gujarati lifestyles from puritan asceticism to conspicuous consumption, in recent years the dominance of the Marathi middle classes in Bombay cricket has been well-nigh complete.

This transition from Parsi/Gujarati to Maharashtrian dominance is exemplified by the shift in Bombay's cricketing headquarters that took place in the early seventies. Without a home of its own, the Bombay Cricket Association (BCA) hosted its Test matches at the Brabourne Stadium of the Cricket Club of India (CCI). When the elite CCI—whose managing committee included the venerable Vijay Merchant— refused to allot a greater number of tickets to the BCA, the latter organization decided to build its own stadium. Named for the long-time president of the BCA and a sometime minister in the State Government of Maharashtra, the Wankhede Stadium was commissioned in 1975, consigning the wonderfully appointed Brabourne to the ash-heap of cricket history.

What knits together these two cultures are the three tiers of competitive cricket in the city.* At the top of the pyramid are the two tournaments for full-fledged adults: the Kanga League for private clubs, and the Times of India Shield for offices and companies. As the Kanga League is played in the monsoon, the Times Shield is conducted in the winter. This temporal sequence permits double affiliations, so that Ajit Wadekar could play for Shivaji Park Gymkhana and State Bank of India, Dilip Vengsarkar for Dadar Union and Tatas.

Club cricket in Bombay is extraordinarily competitive, so it came as a shock when Bishen Bedi, as manager of a losing Indian team in New Zealand, claimed his side lost because they batted as if 'it was not a one-day international but the Kanga League'. Not for the first time, the Sardar of Spin was speaking through his sea-green *patka*. For the Kanga League, played in the monsoon, on green wickets, has been singularly responsible for the marvellous technique Bombay batsmen have had while playing swing bowling. Dilip Vengsarkar's three successive centuries in Lord's Tests, and the fine records Vijay Merchant, Vijay Manjrekar and Sunil Gavaskar have had in England, all owe something to the city's premier tournament.

Of course, Yorkshire too has traditionally relied on club cricket, notably the Bradford League, to throw up players of quality for the county team. However, Maharashtrians being somewhat more book-minded, many of Bombay's cricketers, unlike those of Yorkshire, have had under family pressure to acquire a college degree. Consequently, college cricket has

* See Richard Cashman, Patrons, Players and the Crowd: The Phenomenon of Indian Cricket (Orient Longman, 1980).

33

always been of near first class standard, with the Elphinstone–St Xavier's rivalry being replaced at a later date by the Poddar–Ruia one. Umrigar, Phadkar and Modi of an earlier generation, and Shastri and Patil more recently, first made their mark in college and university cricket.

Finally, there are the inter-school tournaments for the Giles and Harris shields. Following mammoth scores in the Harris Shield, Sachin Tendulkar was catapulted into the Bombay Ranji Trophy side, and after only one season there, into the Indian Test team. Likewise, Sunil Gavaskar and Ashok Mankad built steadily on cricketing reputations first acquired in inter-school competition. It is to one of Bombay's greatest schoolboy cricketers, Eknath Solkar, that we now turn.

III

When a game is as deeply embedded in a local culture as cricket is in Bombay, its most distinctive personalities are not necessarily its greatest performers. For Neville Cardus, it was a player with a modest first class record, Emmot Robinson, who exemplified the traditions of Yorkshire cricket far more than Herbert Sutcliffe or Leonard Hutton. Likewise, I have always held Eknath Solkar, rather than Sunil Gavaskar or Dilip Vengsarkar, to be the embodiment of Bombay cricket. Solkar epitomized the quiet courage and thorough professionalism of the island city's cricket, just as G.R. Viswanath epitomized the gaiety of Karnataka and Mohinder Amarnath the never-say-die spirit of the Punjabi.

Solkar's own biography is deeply interwoven with the history of Bombay cricket. To understand the man and his game we must go back to 1890, the year a grey eminence of the Marylebone Cricket Club assumed one of the most powerful posts in the British Empire, the Governorship of the Bombay

Presidency. This was Lord Harris, captain of Kent, a former President of MCC, and, with his fellow peer Lord Hawke of Yorkshire, indisputably one of the most powerful men in English cricket—the two were referred to, with affection and awe, as the Archbishops of Canterbury and York.

Harris stayed but five years in Bombay. On his return to England he was immediately at the centre of a controversy involving the first great Indian cricketer, Kumar Shri Ranjitsinhji. Harris was influential in the MCC's decision to leave out Ranji from the 1896 season's first Test match, against Australia at Lord's. While the press and public strongly supported Ranji's inclusion (the Australians themselves had made it clear they had no objection), Harris opposed it on the grounds that the Sussex batsman was Indian by birth. Defying the MCC, the Lancashire committee chose Ranji for the next Test at Old Trafford, where the prince made a memorable debut, scoring 62 and 154 not out in a match Australia won.

Notwithstanding his treatment of Ranji, Harris's place in Indian cricket history is secure, for he played a critical part in the creation of the Bombay Pentangular. As Governor he initiated a yearly match between the Europeans of Bombay Presidency and the Parsis, the first Indian community to take to cricket. Then he helped set aside sites for cricket fields on the sea front for the city's three major communities. Around these sites grew the Parsi, Muslim and Hindu Gymkhanas, each of which was responsible for the selection of its community's team in the Pentangular.*

In its early years the Hindu team was beset by a controversy over the inclusion of two gifted cricketers of Untouchable descent, the brothers Palwankar Baloo and Palwankar Vithal. Gandhi and Ambedkar had not yet arrived to challenge the

* See J.D. Coldham, Lord Harris (Allen and Unwin, 1982).

caste system and its treatment of Untouchables, and the balance of opinion was weighted against the inclusion of the brothers. To its lasting credit, the Hindu Gymkhana decided to select them, and the brothers went on to form the nucleus of a strong Hindu side in the nineteen-tens and twenties. A left-handed batsman, Vithal held the middle order together, while Baloo was the first in the line of great Indian left-arm spinners, a worthy forerunner of Mankad and Bedi. Two other brothers, Shivaram and Ganpat, also played for the Hindus, and Ganpat accompanied Baloo on the 1911 tour of England by an All India side. In time, Baloo's son, Yeshwant Palwankar, emerged as a fine all-round cricketer who captained Combined Universities against the West Indies in 1948–9.

More than a century later, and long after the Pentangular was abolished, the Hindu Gymkhana was to make another notable contribution to Indian cricket, in the person of Eknath Dhondu Solkar. Unlike Baloo and Vithal, Solkar was of high-caste origin, but he too came from a lower-class background. He learnt all his cricket at the Hindu Gymkhana, where his father happened to be the groundsman. As a left-handed all-rounder Solkar combined the skills of the Palwankar brothers, though he will be best remembered as the finest fieldsman to be capped for India.

Working his way through the Harris Shield and the Cooch Behar inter-state trophy for schools, 'Ekki' then made his mark as a left-arm spinner for Indian Schoolboys, but the presence of the spin quartet of Bedi, Chandrasekhar, Prasanna and Venkataraghavan persuaded him to try the new ball. (Ironically, Solkar's first coach was Vinoo Mankad—who had himself started as a left-arm seamer and switched to spin only on the advice of his coach, A.F. Wensley.) Although for the most part his role as a Test bowler was strictly ceremonial, preparatory to the advent of Bedi in either the third or fifth over of the innings, Solkar did claim eighteen Test wickets. And he will go to his pyre in the knowledge that he was the particular tormentor of one of the greatest of modern batsmen, Geoffrey Boycott, whom he dismissed six times in seven innings on the 1974 tour of England.

As a batsman Ekki was a fluent strokeplayer, the centrepiece of an aggressive trio which enlivened the lower-middle order of the first (and most likely the last) Indian side to win three Test series in a row. In the first Test I watched, at New Delhi in late 1972, the trio—Farokh Engineer, Solkar and Abid Ali—hit the only three fifties for the home side. After Geoff Arnold had decimated the Indian top order on the first morning of the match, Abid hit a typically pugnacious 58. In the second innings it was the turn of Engineer and Solkar to figure in a thrilling century partnership for the sixth wicket, after the top order had again caved in to the English attack. Solkar was last out for 75, enough to win him a television set for making the highest score of the match.

Like his soulmates Farokh and Abid, Ekki hooked, cut and drove with gusto, and when Wadekar's side finally fell he stood alone among the ruins—a defiant 18 not out in India's lowest ever Test score of 42 at Lord's in 1974. A selfless team man, on occasion he opened for India, and his only Test hundred was made in that pivotal position in the batting order, number three. This was in the last match of possibly the most exciting series played on Indian soil, against West Indies in 1974–5. The teams had come to the newly built Wankhede Stadium all square at two matches apiece, and after winning the toss Lloyd and his men ran up the huge score of 605. On the third afternoon, after their Bombay teammate Engineer had fallen without scoring, Gavaskar and Solkar enchanted the crowd with some superlative strokeplay. Gavaskar now played one of the most brilliant innings of his career, unfolding, as he so rarely did, his array of strokes against the pace of Roberts and Holder and the spin of Gibbs and Barrett. It is no exaggeration to say that on this day Solkar matched the great man stroke for stroke, going on to complete his century on the fourth morning after Gavaskar had fallen, cutting Gibbs, in the last over of the previous day.

Like the man he displaced in the Indian team, Rusi Surti, Solkar was known affectionately as the poor man's Sobers, but in at least one department, fielding, his skills equalled the maestro's. Like Gary he fielded at short leg, though unlike him he sported a blue cap (Sobers was always bare-headed.) With another left-hander, Tony Lock—who was both bare-headed and bald—they were without doubt the finest short legs in the history of the game, and all played before helmets and shin guards were to rob close fielding of some of its dangers, though none of its thrills. Ekki stood out among a gaggle of brilliant close-in fielders—the others were Venkat, Abid and Wadekar, with the ebullient Engineer behind the stumps—who adorned the Indian side of the early seventies. Throughout his career Solkar averaged nearly two catches per Test, a 'clasp rate' matched only by that slip fielder nonpareil, Australia's Bobby Simpson. But he was a marvellous outfielder as well, swift of foot and with a powerful arm. While his confidence in his own ability enabled Solkar to stand a foot closer at short leg than anyone before or since, it also led, unwittingly, to one of the most crucial missed catches in India's Test history, at Port of Spain in 1976. As West Indies struggled to save the match, their captain and anchor Clive Lloyd top-edged Venkat high into the off side. Going for the catch, Solkar, fielding as twelfth man, bumped into an equally eager Brijesh Patel, and the chance was spilled. Ironically, Solkar was on the field only for that one over, while Chandrasekhar had gone off to change his bootlaces. Lloyd didn't make another mistake, batting on to save the match. Ever quick to turn on their heroes, for once Indian fans did not know whom to blame, for if Patel was by far the finest fielder in the playing side, Solkar was better still. In the event, both were forgiven when India won the next Test by scoring more than four hundred in the fourth innings.

The critic Rajan Bala once wrote that their playing gifts had enabled many Indian cricketers to escape from the 'annonymity of clerical serfdom'. That is certainly true of the international stars who have emerged from the middle class Maharashtrian neighbourhoods of central Bombay: products of the two clubs that have dominated the city's cricket in recent decades, Dadar Union and Shivaji Park Gymkhana. Son of a groundsman, Solkar emerged from more lowly origins still. But his cricketing antecedents were even more honourable than those of Vijay Manjrekar (Shivaji Park) and Sunil Gavaskar (Dadar Union), for he came from one of the Gymkhanas that had laid the foundations of Bombay and indeed Indian cricket.

It is sometimes said that Solkar, because of his versatile gifts, would have excelled at the limited-overs game. True, but unlike the bulk of India's present one day side, he was emphatically not a 'bits-and-pieces' cricketer. A batsman of courage and skill and a fielder of genius, Ekki was a player of true international class who exemplified the best in Bombay cricket. Modest and retiring to a fault, no one has more richly deserved the climb up from 'serfdom' brought about by his cricketing gifts.

IV

Despite his fielding and bowling skills, Solkar was happiest with a bat in his hand, and so it has always been in Bombay. When those gifted spinners Prasanna and Chandrasekhar were at their peak, their team, Karnataka (then Mysore) met Bombay in a Ranji Trophy semifinal. The Mysore skipper V. Subrahmanyam implored his batsmen: 'Please get me 300 runs and with our bowlers we will win the match.' As Subrahmanyam himself led the way with a brilliant 125 (five 6s and fifteen 4s), Mysore made 350, but the craft of Prasanna and Chandrasekhar notwithstanding, the left-handed Ajit Wadekar got 323 off his own bat: such has been the awesome strength of the Bombay batting. With a line of Test batsmen that stretches far into the Arabian Sea, and who have collectively scored more than 50,000 Test runs, how does one choose among them for an all-time Bombay XI?

At least there can be no dispute about the openers. The only difficulty is whom to give first strike, Merchant or Gavaskar. By custom, the better (or sometimes, more senior) opener gets to face the first ball. But how does one discriminate between the man whom C.B. Fry wanted to paint white and take to Australia with the English team, and the only player to have scored more than 10,000 runs in Test cricket? But this, as we shall presently see, is a minor matter. Number three through five are the real problem. Whom to drop (and choose) among Vijay Manjrekar, Polly Umrigar, Ajit Wadekar, Rusi Modi and Dilip Vengsarkar, not to speak of L.P. Jai, Dilip Sardesai, Ashok Mankad, Sandeep Patil and Sanjay Manjrekar? My own preferences—as an outsider, of course—run to Vijay Manjrekar, an outstanding player of spin bowling who alone with Vijay Hazare defied Trueman when Fiery Fred went wild in the series of 1952; Polly Umrigar who, despite an aversion to real pace decimated most attacks and whose Test record speaks for itself; and Dilip Vengsarkar, that most highly regarded of modern batsmen. However, with this choice Bombay would be well advised to have Eknath Solkar or Ramnath Parkar handy to field as substitutes for Vijay Manjrekar and Vijay Merchant, both players an embarrassment even at the pension points of

mid on and third man. Leaving Wadekar out has been especially painful. Apart from being the only left-hander of the lot,
he was a relentless accumulator; at the Ranji Trophy level,
possibly as run hungry as Gavaskar himself.

There is a story told of Ranji and Fry that bears repeating
here. At the height of their powers, they batted numbers 3 and
4 for Sussex, following the workmanlike pair of Vine and
Killick. According to the Yorkshire pro Ted Wainwright (a
Cardus favourite who once complained that Ranji 'never
played a Christian stroke in his life') when Sussex were batting
the rest of the side could just as well go to nearby Brighton
beach and bathe. Well, Indians have never fancied the water,
but with a batting line up which begins Gavaskar, Merchant,
Manjrekar, Umrigar and Vengsarkar, surely numbers six
through eleven could do the next best thing and go off to
Chowpatti beach and eat *bhelpuri.*

V

Not that the choice of bowlers is any easier. For the new ball,
at least three right-arm-left-arm combinations present themselves for consideration. First, Dattu Phadkar and Karsan
Ghavri. Phadkar had the impressive number of 62 Test wickets
at a time when internationals were few and far between, wickets
true, and Indian captains as partial to spin as in the sixties. A
fine swing bowler, Dattu's bowling fell away—as did that of
some other Indian pacemen—after he went through Alf Gover's
school in 1952, but fortunately his batting developed around
the same time. Whereas Phadkar was to eventually leave his
native Bombay for Bengal and the Railways, Karsan Ghavri
came to the city as a young man from humble beginnings in the
Gujarat town of Rajkot. In an era of more frequent Tests,
Ghavri garnered 109 wickets, slanting the ball away from the

41

right-hand batsman from left-arm over the wicket, though many of his wickets came from a wicked bouncer that was—or so it appeared—twice as fast as his normal delivery. Kapil Dev and Karsan Ghavri formed the most dangerous new ball pair to play for India since Nissar and Amar Singh, and, like Kapil, Ghavri was no rabbit with the bat, being especially severe, with his whirling backlift, on slow bowlers.

The finest Bombay fast bowler since Phadkar has been the large-hearted Ramakant Desai. Despite his diminutive stature—he was barely five foot four in his socks—Desai was quick enough on Indian wickets to disconcert the great Hanif Mohammad, whom he dismissed with unfailing regularity during the series of 1960-1. A man of rare courage, 'Tiny' Desai scored 32 not out, batting with a broken jaw, to help India to its first overseas Test victory, over New Zealand in 1968. The left-armer who bowled with Desai for Bombay and India was the tall and rangy Ghulam Guard, a city policeman. (When Guard had Gary Sobers caught and bowled in a Bombay Test, a wag remarked: 'that's the most famous arrest he'll ever make.') Our third pair, G.S. Ramchand and E.D. Solkar, lag somewhat behind the other two in terms of bowling ability, but their fielding and batting skills make up for any deficiencies in that regard.

At first glance the spinners pick themselves rather more easily. We must of course begin with Subhas Gupte, the leg-spinner who was master of a craft of which the last days were not yet upon us. Unlike parsimonious Yorkshire, Bombay has produced many fine wrist-spinners, but Subhas was far and away the best of the lot. Fine bowler though he is, Abdul Qadir's powers are greatly magnified by the lack of competition and the unfamiliarity of most modern batsmen with this form of attack—I cannot believe he is as good a bowler as Gupte was. Ask those who have seen both. Better still, ask Gary

Sobers, who said more than once that 'Fergie' Gupte gave him as much trouble as any bowler in international cricket.

Gupte had, in fact, a lasting connection with the Caribbean. His nickname came from the West Indies leg-spinner W. Ferguson who toured India with John Goddard's side in 1948–9. Gupte had the Indian sign on a whole generation of West Indian batsmen, and his 26 wickets in the 1952–3 series in the islands is a performance unequalled by a visiting spinner. Fittingly, he married a girl from Trinidad and settled down there.

A famous story is told of how Gupte, after dismissing Rohan Kanhai several times in succession, walked up to the little West Indian on the morning of a Calcutta Test and greeted him with 'hello, rabbit'. As Kanhai's answer was to score 256, this story is generally told against Gupte. I am not so sure. To me, Fergie's bravado signified an abundance of self-confidence, without which no spin bowler can survive in international cricket. As much as fast bowlers, spinners need to have faith in their own abilities, and if two recent slow bowlers, Shivlal Yadav and L. Sivaramakrishnan, had some of Subhas's confidence, they'd be playing Test cricket yet.

In cricketing folklore Gupte's success was in large measure due to an almost magical sleight of hand. V.M. Muddiah, who played Test cricket with Subhas, remembers fielding in his leg trap on the 1959 tour of England. At leg slip, Muddiah watched Gupte's hand so as to know when to be alerted to the googly, and a possible inside edge towards him. 'Forget it', said Bapu Nadkarni, fielding next door at short square leg, 'Just watch the batsman—I play with Gupte for Bombay and still can't read him.' His experiences alongside the wrist-spinner led Muddiah to remark: 'If Gupte had had half as much support in the field as [the Australian leg-spinner] Richie Benaud, he would have got four times as many Test wickets.' Some confirmation for

43

these nationalist sentiments comes from a man whose place in cricketing history rests in part on his famous battles with Benaud: Frankie Worrell, who told Fred Trueman that Gupte was by far the best leg-spinner he had played against.

When Gupte first played for India, Vinoo Mankad had fourteen years of international cricket behind him. Despite being a finger spinner, Vinoo had as much variation as Subhas. Mankad was so crafty, recalled the West Indian batsman Jeff Stollmeyer, that after bowling his arm ball he would run away to the off side as if expecting turn. He was, in addition, a marvellous fielder off his own bowling—according to one contemporary, so good that mid-on and mid-off could stand at least eight yards wider than usual.

Mankad's greatest triumphs came in the year of India's first General Election, 1952. In February he bowled India to its first Test victory, over England at Madras, with figures of 38.5/15/55/8 and 30.4/9/53/4. Throughout that series Mankad had bowled magnificently—as Wisden remarked, he was 'by far the best bowler on either side'. Late in the year, with Jawaharlal Nehru's elected government firmly ensconced, Mankad spearheaded India to its first series win over Pakistan. In the two Tests India won, Mankad took thirteen and nine wickets respectively; when he missed the Lucknow Test through illness, India lost by an innings.

Like Wilfred Rhodes before him and Bishen Bedi since, Mankad knew you could never flight a ball, only an over. In his remarkable spell of 8 for 55, on the first day of a Test on a plumb Chepauk wicket, Mankad came up against England's best batsmen, J.D. Robertson and Tom Graveney, both well set. To Robertson Vinoo bowled four balls on a perfect length, to all of which Robertson played defensively. The fifth was slightly shorter and faster, and even as Robertson came on his forward defensive prod, Vinoo was at silly mid-off to complete an amazing caught and bowled. To Graveney, Mankad bowled a series of beautifully flighted deliveries, each an inch further away from the off stump. Finally Graveney was dragged out of his crease searching for the ball, and P. Sen had one of his five stumpings of the match.

Wickets are wickets, but Mankad probably treasured as much the bouquets he garnered from the great spin bowlers of the game. On the 1947 tour of Australia, that millionaire of wrist-spin, Arthur Mailey, hailed him as 'unquestionably' the world's best left-arm spinner, noting that Mankad had bowled better Down Under than had England's Hedley Verity. But the crowning tribute had come Mankad's way on the England tour of the previous year, from none other than Wilfred Rhodes. When India played Yorkshire at Bradford, Mankad had come with a considerable reputation. Rhodes, Maurice Leyland and other Yorkshire greats were watching keenly, and as John Arlott wrote, a 'respectful whisper went round the ground. There were no hasty conclusions, they watched long and intently, missing nothing: Mankad passed the toughest critical school in England—probably the world.'

Despite the massive difference in age, Mankad and Gupte bowled in harness in Test series in West Indies and Pakistan, for Bombay in the early fifties, and for Rajasthan towards the end of the decade. Gupte was very much a Bombay product, although he played one season for Bengal in between and moved to Rajasthan in his declining years. One of the first cricketers to be registered as a professional with the Board, Mankad played for at least six states, including Bengal and Gujarat, but I want to reserve him for the state where he spent his boyhood and early cricketing career, Nawanagar.*

---

* Two of Mankad's sons, Ashok and Rahul, both of whom were batsmen, played only for Bombay. A veteran of twenty-two Tests, Ashok was highly regarded as a cricket tactician, and led Bombay to more than one Ranji triumph.

Another of our choices, Vijay Manjrekar, also played for six states, but like Gupte he was born in Bombay and spent his formative years in the city.)

With Mankad unavailable, we can still call upon one of four left-arm spinners who have played for India—the Parsis R.J. Jamshedji and Keki Tarapore (one Test each), and the more enduring Bapu Nadkarni and R.J. Shastri. Ahead of these Test cricketers one must pick Padmakar Shivalkar—unlike Bapu and Shastri, an attacking bowler. Kept out for many years by the versatile Nadkarni—Shivalkar could not bat and was an indifferent field—he had to wait till he was thirty to make his first-class debut. Thereafter his path to the Indian side was blocked by the ample figure of Bishen Bedi. (Incidentally, who would one judge to be the most cruelly hit by fate: the left-armers Shivalkar and Rajinder Goel for overlapping with Bedi, the googly bowlers V.V. Kumar and C.G. Joshi for being around when Chandrasekhar was, or the off-spinners Nausher Mehta and Uday Joshi for having Prasanna and Venkat as contemporaries?) Even so, Shivalkar shouldered the Bombay attack for more than a dozen years, and to at least ten Ranji championships. In 1988, at the age of forty-seven, he was recalled to the Bombay side for the quarter-final with Karnataka. There he accounted for a mere lad of thirty-nine also in his last season of first class cricket, G.R. Viswanath.

In keeping with Indian tradition, an all-time Bombay XI must also have three spinners. For balance, an off-spinner would do nicely, and the chiefs of this tribe in Bombay have been S.J. (Jimmy) Diwadkar, and his brother-in-law (and Gavaskar's closest friend) Milind Rege. There are, too, some wrist-spinners to take account of, notably Subhas Gupte's younger brother Baloo, and Sadashiv Shinde, who first played for Maharashtra but ended up in Bombay. A considerable success in the Ranji Trophy, Baloo failed in the two Tests he played, while Shinde—who died tragically at thirty-two—was good enough to get six wickets on the first day of a Test match against England at the Ferozeshah Kotla in 1951.* (But for a dozen dropped catches, Shinde would most likely have got six in the second innings too.)

The most convenient solution would be to ask the broad shouldered Polly Umrigar to shed some batting responsibility and concentrate on his medium-paced off-breaks, as he did while helping Jasu Patel to India's first Test win over Australia, at Kanpur in 1959–60. We can then smuggle in one more batsman, a toss-up between Rusi Modi (style) and Ajit Wadekar (solidity).

VI

The embarrassment of riches troubles us to the last. For we now have to choose between several wicket-keepers, each with a long and distinguished record at the international level. Almost on par with the lineage of opening batsmen and left-arm spinners, the Bombay tradition of wicket-keeping starts with Bahadur Kapadia, the ageless captain of the Parsis in the Pentangular. Kapadia toured England in 1932, by which time he was past his prime. His place in the Bombay side was taken by D.D. 'Darfu' Hindlekar, who toured England in 1936 and 1946. Equally at home to the spin of Vinoo Mankad and the pace of Mohammed Nissar, Hindlekar also won critical acclaim for his skill in taking the brisk medium-pace of Lala Amarnath from over the stumps. Hindlekar is one of the very few cricketers to have opened the innings and batted number eleven in different Tests. This was on the 1946 tour, when his

---

* Shinde's son-in-law, Sharad Pawar, formerly Chief Minister of Maharashtra State, based in Bombay, is now Union Defence Minister.

resolute defence with the bat (to be expected of an uncle of Vijay Manjrekar) helped save the Old Trafford Test.

Hindlekar was succeeded by Madhav Mantri. Now better known as Sunil Gavaskar's maternal uncle, Mantri was in his playing days a capable wicket-keeper-batsman and one of Bombay's shrewdest cricket brains. He in turn gave way to Naren Tamhane, who as an old fashioned wicket-keeper was seldom heard and never seen. But his skills did not escape the eagle-eyed Vijay Merchant, who once said that Tamhane was as safe as the Bank of England—no mean praise from an industrialist who knew the working of banks intimately. Tamhane was particularly adept at taking his Bombay team-mate Subhas Gupte, something which went in his favour when his place in the Test side was challenged by P. Sen of Bengal or Maharashtra's P.G. 'Nana' Joshi.

Tamhane was never known to dive: perhaps he never needed to. Unlike his predecessor, Farokh Engineer was a compulsive diver who ran up a huge laundry bill. His flamboyance—both behind and before the sticks—and sunny personality helped make 'Farokhy' one of the best loved cricketers of his time. Now settled in Lancashire, his devotion to Indian cricket is undiminished. Handed the mike by his fellow BBC commentators at the moment India won the 1983 World Cup, Engineer could only mutter, 'Incredible! Incredible!...', emerging only to call upon Mrs Indira Gandhi to declare a national holiday. It is indeed sad to reflect that Farokhy was probably the last Parsi to have played cricket for Bombay and India.

VII

Having been bold enough to put together an all-time eleven, I do not think I can dare visit Bombay again. To mollify my friends from that city (if such a thing is possible) I have also

BOMBAY'S BEST—THREE (AND A HALF) GENERATIONS

1. Sanjay's father 2. Sunny Tonny 3. The Invisible Hands (from PJ Hindu Gymkhana) 4. Vijay's son 5. The boy 6. Bombay's Good European 7. Polly, the Pride of the Parsis 8. Bapu, the King of the Maiden Over 9. The India captain from Shivaji Park 10. Champion of Champions 11. Lord of Lord's

presented a Bombay second eleven quite as good as the first eleven of any other state. However, if my friends in Dadar—I do not have any left in Shivaji Park—would want to interchange Ghavri with Desai, Wadekar with Modi, or Engineer with Tamhane, I can have no objection.

All Time Bombay XI	Alternate All Time Bombay XI
1. S.M. Gavaskar	1. M.L. Apte
2. V.M. Merchant (captain)	2. D.N. Sardesai
3. V.L. Manjrekar	3. A.L. Wadekar
4. D.B. Vengsarkar	4. L.P. Jai (captain)
5. R.S. Modi	5. Sanjay Manjrekar
6. P.R. Umrigar	6. G.S. Ramchand
7. D.G. Phadkar	7. R.G. Nadkarni
8. N. Tamhane (wicket-keeper)	8. F.M. Engineer (wicket-keeper)
9. R.B. Desai	9. K.D. Ghavri
10. S.P. Gupte	10. R.J. Jamshedji
11. P.D. Shivalkar	11. S.G. Shinde
12th man: E.D. Solkar	12th man: R.D. Parkar

Only one thing remains to be said. As the age of decolonization is upon us, and given Bombay's infinitely greater staying powers—as I write Yorkshire are bottom of the county championship, which they haven't won since 1968—would it not be more just to call Yorkshire 'England's Bombay'?

50

CHAPTER THREE

The Lions of Punjab
– in Delhi

The crown is gradually slipping from the head of Bombay Presidency
and the robust Panjabis are well nigh threatening to wrest the
championship honours from [them].

Prithviraj, Punjab cricketer, in 1939.

rchitecturally speaking, India's capital is dominated by the buildings of two imperial cities: the
columned offices and colonial bungalows of New
Delhi and the Mughal forts and mosques of Old
Delhi. Ferozeshah Kotla, the epicentre of Delhi cricket, neatly
straddles these two magnificent creations. Thus, when Vivian
Richards, in his imperial innings of 192 not out in the Delhi
Test of 1974, struck the off-spinner Venkataraghavan into the
adjoining Ambedkar football stadium, he had, in a manner of
speaking, sent the ball all the way from New Delhi to Old Delhi.

Neither the city of Lutyens' creation nor the older city of
the Mughals has, however, contributed significantly to the
capital's cricketing ethos. For until very recently, Delhi's Ranji
Trophy team relied heavily on a seemingly unending flow of
university stars, from the campus to the north of the old city.
The annual clash between the two top colleges of Delhi
University, Hindu and St Stephen's, attracted far greater

51

crowds than the more famous encounters between Oxford and Cambridge—besides, the cricket was, at least since the late fifties, of a consistently higher quality. Having distinguished themselves at the university level, the stars of college cricket made the progression to the first-class game. This transition was greatly facilitated by the availability, within the capital, of a plethora of turf wickets. Whereas cricketers in Bangalore, Hyderabad and Madras—to name only three cities—have to make do for the most part with matting wickets, the cricketers of Delhi and Bombay have been fortunate in having access, from an early age, to the surface on which the game is played at the highest level.

The high quality of university cricket has served the capital well. College cricketers who have gone on to represent Delhi (and, in some cases, India) with distinction include Prem Bhatia, Manmohan Sood, Rajinder Pal, Ashok Gandotra, Michael Dalvi, Arun Lal, Raman Lamba, Sunil Valson and Manoj Prabhakar. While this reservoir of talent enabled Delhi to be comfortably ahead of other teams in the North Zone, somehow the highest honours eluded it. For Delhi to make a serious bid for the Ranji Trophy, two things had to happen. First, the focus had to shift from the college to the school. Taking a cue from their counterparts in Bombay, cricket coaches in Delhi started working on the principle of 'catch them young'. This policy has paid handsome dividends, and for more than two decades now Delhi Schools has been a team feared by schoolboys across the land. In this transformation, coaches such as Gursharan Singh and Tarak Sinha have come to enjoy a status similar to that enjoyed in Bombay by the likes of V.S. Patil and Vasu Paranjype.

II

The real transformation in Delhi cricket, however, occurred only through an infusion of talent from outside the capital. As is well known, the economy of India's capital city rests on an edifice painstakingly built by post-Partition migrants from Punjab. But there has been, in recent years, another migration from Punjab, whose impact on the capital's cricket has been even more momentous. Led by Bishen Singh Bedi, the stream of Punjabi exiles which has nourished Delhi cricket includes the two Amarnaths—Mohinder and Surinder—and Madan Lal. A fifth exile, welcomed as eagerly in the Kotla and whose contribution to Delhi cricket has been as critical, came from the west—Maharashtra's Chetan Chauhan. (Chauhan, a cricketer with an acute sense of history, could point out that he drew inspiration from an even earlier migration—for the Marathas had begun exploring around Delhi as long ago as the eighteenth century!)

Bedi's feats with the ball are legendary. While he did not fare as well as captain in the combative world of Test cricket, he worked wonders with the Delhi team. He commanded absolute loyalty, and younger members of the side only spoke of him in hushed tones. When he moved to Delhi from Punjab in 1968, the Sardar of Spin was assigned by his employers, the State Bank of India, to their Tis Hazari branch; an appropriate location, for Tis Hazari is exactly halfway between Delhi University and Ferozeshah Kotla. Bedi quickly took young college cricketers in hand, shepherding dozens into the Delhi Ranji Trophy side and at least four to full international status.

Bedi led from the front, and the others followed. There was no more loyal follower than that doughty all-rounder, Madan Lal Sharma. Like his mentor, Madan Lal studied at the P.B.N. Higher Secondary School and Hindu College at Amritsar, where he was shaped by Bedi's own coach, Gian Prakash. At the international level, Madan earned a reputation, not wholly undeserved, for retreating towards square leg against fast bowling; on the slower Indian wickets, and against spin, he was an altogether different proposition. His Ranji Trophy record speaks for itself, and on more than one occasion, with Delhi behind on the first innings, Madan has led a victorious fightback with both bat and ball.

Although he once took five wickets in an innings of a miserably cold Test at Christchurch, Madan's successes in Test cricket were mostly on the slower (and dustier) Indian wickets. Along with Kapil Dev he bowled India to victory on the last day of a Bombay Test, when, in foxing Keith Fletcher's Englishmen with a spell of ever lower off-cutters, he put to good use the experience of playing alongside Abid Ali in his first days as an international player. He probably treasures most the part he played in India's last Test victory against England, at Leeds in 1986. With Chetan Sharma injured, the Indian selectors were unwilling to blood the inexperienced Manoj Prabhakar and called up Madan from the Lancashire Leagues. At the close of the first day, India were precariously placed at 235 for 9, and the English press rubbed their hands with glee at what Gower, Gatting and company would do to an Indian attack which included 'dear old Madan Lal'. Madan responded magnificently, clean bowling Slack and Smith and, with Kapil again, helping India to a first innings lead of over a hundred, the platform for a comfortable victory. The ageless all-rounder also played two vital innings of twenty odd in this low scoring match, and even effected a brilliant run out.

Madan was here carrying on a remarkable tradition of Indian touring teams in England calling on cricketers from professional duties in Lancashire. This tradition started in 1936 when Amar Singh—the first Indian professional to play in the Lancashire Leagues—was released by his club, Colne, to lead India's attack in the three Tests of that year. Sixteen years later, Vinoo Mankad's club, Rochdale, released him to play in the Lord's Test after India had been soundly beaten in the first Test at Headingley. (In a game known to posterity simply as 'Mankad's Match', Vinoo scored 72 and 184 opening the batting, and took 5 for 196 in 73 overs in England's first innings.) Then, in 1971, the wicket-keeper-batsman Farokh Engineer was requisitioned—not from the Leagues but from the Lancashire County Cricket Club itself—to play a crucial role in India's first series win in England. Amar Singh, Mankad, Engineer: three names to conjure with, and while Madan Lal isn't in the same league as a cricketer, no one had a bigger heart.

III

In this most violent of centuries, war and civil strife have frequently uprooted entire communities. In our own subcontinent, millions of Punjabis, Sindhis and Bengalis have had to rebuild their lives, sometimes more than once, literally from scratch. But Madan Lal's long-time new ball partner for Delhi, Mohinder Amarnath, has had to remake his Test career no less than seven times. For him, the whims of the Indian cricket selectors have been as unpredictable and cruel as the ironies of history against which his fellow Punjabis have so heroically battled.

Mohinder was first picked for India as an eighteen-year-old, in the last Test of the series of 1969–70 against Bill Lawry's Australians. Despite bowling and batting with a maturity well beyond his years, he did not play another Test till 1976. In between, he had been picked for the 1971 tour of England, only to be sidelined when Engineer's unavailability for the county matches forced the selectors to take along Kirmani as the third wicket-keeper. When at last picked, for the twin tour of New Zealand and the West Indies, Mohinder batted impressively in the middle order. Yet one failure at Delhi against England the next winter, and he was dropped for the rest of the series. Recalled for the tour of Australia in 1977–8, he scored one hundred and three fifties, batting at number 3. For older Australians, his hooking of Jeff Thomson brought back memories of his father, who, thirty years earlier, had played a series of memorable innings against the state sides (though unlike the Lala, Mohinder came good in the Test matches as well).

His penchant for the hook, however, cost Mohinder dearly in the three Test series in Pakistan the next winter. Dropped for the first four matches of the home series against a West Indies side badly truncated by Kerry Packer, he made a century when recalled for the Kanpur Test. Early on in next summer's tour of England, he was laid out cold by Richard Hadlee. By now, he had acquired a reputation for being uncertain against the bouncer. The helmet had just come into vogue, but the Lala angrily refused to allow his son to wear one. Accordingly, he appeared in the last Test against Australia in Bombay in 1979 wearing a *sola topee*. When Rodney Hogg predictably greeted him with a bouncer, Mohinder trod on his wicket, also losing his *topee* in the process.

At the time, it seemed that the Bombay fiasco had effectively finished the younger Amarnath's international career. Yet he continued to pile up the runs in domestic cricket, and three years later found himself in the train to Pakistan. By this time the Lala had thankfully relented, and the helmet played no mean part in Mohinder's resounding success. With six hundred runs in that series (which India lost 3-0) and a similar aggregate in the series in the Caribbean that followed, Mohinder had established himself as the best player of fast bowling in the world. He went on to star with both bat and ball in India's World Cup win, claiming man-of-the-match awards in semi-final and final. Yet on his return he inexplicably lost form, scoring but one run in 6 innings against the West Indians (this was the one occasion on which Mohinder deserved to be dropped, and he was). Since then, he continued to be treated like a yo-yo —recalled for the 1986 tour of England, dropped for next year's World Cup, reinstated for the home series against the West Indies, dropped again the following winter (when his outburst against the selectors cooked his goose), surprisingly recalled for the Nehru Cup in 1989, and then dropped again, this time for good.

In the midst of his most famous comeback, in Pakistan in 1982-3, Mohinder found himself at the wicket with India 10 for 2, both Gavaskar and Arun Lal having fallen to the rampaging Imran. In one glorious moment, Imran bounced, and Mohinder swung him over square leg for six. His father, as usual the expert on Pakistani television, was beside himself with joy, exclaiming, 'they dropped the boy for three years saying he can't play fast bowling'. But this mastery of Imran and the awesome West Indians should not make us forget that he is a wonderful player of spin bowling as well, inheriting his father's immaculate footwork. Connoisseurs will remember his two lofted drives off Larry Gomes in the World Cup final of 1983, when he countered the off-spinner's drift towards the on and 3-6 field by dancing down and away from the wicket to strike the ball through the comparatively untenanted off side. Mohinder's virtuosity was underscored when that honest craftsman Yashpal Sharma tried the same shot, only to spoon up an easy catch to cover.

In the history of Indian cricket, Mohinder was indisputably the most effective 'breach stopper' not to hail from Bombay. When Mohinder walked in to bat after the fall of an early wicket or two in a Test match, a wave of reassurance swept over his countrymen. As he emerged from the pavilion, 'Jimmy' Amarnath always looked over his shoulder into the sun—a habit characteristic of other Northern players like Chetan Chauhan and Navjyot Sidhu, but one I have never seen resorted to by batsmen from Bombay or the South. Characteristic, too, was the man's gardening style. Meeting the first ball firmly in the middle of the bat, he would walk a few steps, and then, with the handle held loose, put down the offending pieces of turf with the blade at right angles, rather than parallel to, the wicket.

Mohinder was probably as good a batsman at forty—when he was removed from the Indian side on account of his age—as he had been at any stage of his career. In fact, as he grew older his range of strokes widened. Starting out as an on-side player, in time he developed a stunning array of off-side strokes. Like other Indian batsmen (notably Kapil Dev), he exacted a heavy toll off Abdul Qadir, delighting in hitting the wrist-spinner's googly, inside out, over extra cover.

Mohinder's batting gifts were without a doubt inherited from the father. Fifty years before the son scored six hundred runs in a series against the feared West Indies pace quartet, the Lala hit a brilliant hundred in the final of the Moin-ud-Dowla tournament in Hyderabad, displaying a complete mastery over the opposing team's spearhead, Learie Constantine. (Constantine, who bowled bodyline in that match, was so impressed by Amarnath's batting that he invited him to take his place as club professional with Nelson in the Lancashire League.) Again, like his father Mohinder bowled sharp inswingers off a six-step run. Only their temperaments were different. Whereas his middle son, at least until his row with the selectors in 1988, had a most equable manner, the Lala was always (in Mushtaq Ali's wonderful words) 'quick to love and quick to fight'.

For all his success in international cricket, Mohinder has remained in awe of his father. When he and his brother Surinder played for Delhi at Ferozeshah Kotla, the Lala seldom failed to be at the ground. As one of the brothers got out, the father, thoughtfully puffing at his pipe, would follow him into the dressing room. After the Lala would re-emerge, wild rumours would begin circulating among the crowd. 'Tumne suna kya hua? Lalaji ne ek thappad mara bete ko!' (Did you hear what happened? The Lala slapped his son for that bad shot.) Of such flimsy evidence are cricket tales spun, but the boys' devotion to their father was real. When Mohinder finally played a Test at Lord's, he was sought out by the great Denis Compton. 'Did you know', Compton told Mohinder, 'that I played against your father in 1946, and he bowled me for a duck'. 'Yes', replied the son, 'I have often heard about that'. As the writer Robin Marlar observed, this exchange tells us a great deal about all three men—Compton's generosity, the Lala's pride, and his son's devotion.

There is another delightful tale from that 1946 England tour which illustrates the elder Amarnath's pride in his craft. In the match against Somerset, the Lala bowled a series of probing maiden overs to one of the fiercest hitters then in the game, Harold Gimblett. At length the exasperated Gimblett asked the Lala: 'Don't you ever bowl a half volley'. 'Oh yes', replied Amarnath, 'I bowled one in 1940'.

It was only just that Mohinder's greatest innings were played in Pakistan. For the Lala is held in the highest esteem in Lahore, Karachi and a dozen other cricketing cities there, which he graced in pre-Partition days. A wonderful story is told of the arrival of the 1978 Indian team, the first to tour Pakistan in twenty-three years. As the team (which included both Mohinder and Surinder) and its entourage got off the plane, it was met on the tarmac by a bus and a Toyota. As the cricketers and journalists strolled towards the bus, one man strode imperiously towards the car. This was the team's manager, Fathehsinghrao Gaekwad, in his time the ruler of Baroda, art collector, wild-life enthusiast, Member of Parliament and a column of the international jet set. Not surprisingly, the prince assumed the car to be at his disposal. As he approached the Toyota, however, he was shooed away by its liveried chauffeur, who pointed towards the bus and firmly said: 'Tum udhar jao. Ye siraf Lala Saheb ke liye hai' (You go there. This is only for the Lala).*

IV

In character and in cricketing styles, Mohinder and his brother Surinder were as dissimilar as curry and rice (but, as Cardus once remarked of Merchant and Mushtaq Ali, just as effective in combination). In the course of their long and distinguished careers, the brothers batted numbers 3 and 4 for Punjab Schools, Indian Schoolboys, Guru Nanak Dev University, Punjab, Delhi and North Zone. Surinder won lasting fame as captain of an outstanding Indian Schoolboys side which included Eknath Solkar, Syed Kirmani and Dipankar Sarkar, hitting two sixes when his side required ten runs to win off the last two balls of a Lord's international. Where Mohinder was affable and outgoing, Surinder kept very much to himself. Not a natural left-hander but brought up by his canny father to be one, Surinder's most productive strokes were the cut and the pull. (In contrast, Mohinder's game is founded more classi-

* I owe this story to Kishore Bhimani, cricket correspondent of *The Statesman*.

60

cally on the drive.) After a century on debut, his Test record was by no means undistinguished—he was one of the few players to emerge with any credit from the series India lost against England in 1976–7 and Pakistan in 1978—and he could justifiably feel shortchanged by the selectors. Mohinder certainly thought so. Ever since the most famous of his comebacks in 1982, Mohinder, while on the field, sported the red handkerchief which Surinder, and the Lala before him, always had sticking out of a side pocket, as if to say 'this one is for my brother, too'.

To precede the Amarnaths in an all-time Delhi side we can do worse than choose Vijay Mehra, sure in defense; and that member of a distinguished cricketing family, Akash Lal, who was equally sure in attack (both Mehra and Akash, like Bedi and company, were migrants from Punjab). Although the choice is not easy, I prefer the combination of an unorthodox defensive opener, Chetan Chauhan, and an unorthodox attacking opener, Raman Lamba—the latter snuffs out the challenge of his cousin and namesake, Vinay Lamba.

The son of an army officer, Chauhan was coached by Kamal Bhandarkar at Pune's Wadia College, and first played for India against New Zealand in 1969. In the wilderness for half a dozen years, he accepted Bedi's invitation to move northwards. Almost immediately, in a practice match with my college, St. Stephen's, his jaw was broken by our fast bowler. This setback only made him more determined: on a liquid diet for months, he substituted runs for food with such fierceness that he ended the season of 1976-7 with an aggregate of seven hundred runs and a ticket to Australia. A year after being felled by an unknown college bowler, Chauhan was facing Jeff Thomson with scarcely less distinction than the man whose regular partner he was to become, Sunil Gavaskar.

With his low grip and crouching stance, Chauhan was a

formidable defensive batsman, as bowlers of at least five countries were to find out to their cost. His reputation for doggedness preceded him when when he came to practice at the St. Stephen's College nets shortly after his move to Delhi. Imagine our surprise when his stint at the nets ended with a flurry of lofted shots, each accompanied by the invocation, delivered from the side of the mouth, of 'Six to Win! Six to Win!'

This was well before the coming of one-day cricket, and Chauhan was hardly likely to be at the wicket, with six runs to win and only the last ball of a Test match to be bowled. Nonetheless, he had been prepared for this eventuality by Kamal Bhandarkar, who, one may assume, got it in turn from C.K. Nayudu. A man who required no such training was Raman Lamba. Like Kirti Azad, Manmohan Sood and a few other Delhi batsmen, Lamba had—indeed, still has—an outstanding record in domestic cricket, yet he failed at the highest level. He was a close contemporary of mine in college. In inter-college matches I usually got him out, but only after he had helped himself to a liberal dose of fours and sixes at my expense (a typical lunchtime score—PGDAV College 127 for 3, last man (Lamba) 107).

V

Now to the bowling. Madan would be ably partnered by Rajinder Pal, the Hindu College Express who came to the top at a time when the Indian selectors set store exclusively by spin. Poor 'Pali' played only one Test, in which Tiger Pataudi allowed him the luxury of three overs. Fortunately, his services to Indian cricket didn't end there—for he ended his playing days with Haryana, passing on his enormous knowledge of swing and cut to an eager young pupil, Kapil Dev.

Like Bombay, Delhi have been able to call upon a succession of outstanding left-arm spinners. My first college captain and former captain of Indian Schoolboys, Praveen Oberoi, found his way into the Delhi Ranji team blocked by Bedi and the equally formidable Rajinder Goel. Fortunately for Oberoi, Goel moved shortly afterwards to Haryana, but by then he had played a decade with Delhi. Flatter through the air but having even more prodigous powers of spin, Goel was harder to get after than the Sardar, and unplayable on a crumbling wicket. In characteristically generous recognition of these skills, Bedi often brought on Goel first change—that is, before himself—for both Delhi and North Zone. For my money, the leading wicket-taker in the history of the Ranji Trophy must be preferred to the Bedi clone, Maninder Singh, for the second spinner's spot in an all-time Delhi XI.

I could write pages about the Sardar himself (and perhaps will, elsewhere), but for the present I shall restrict myself to one episode and one comment. The very last time I saw Bedi in a first-class match, he was leading Delhi to a comfortable victory over Tamil Nadu, who in the pre-Srikkant days—this was 1979—were a batting side of grace, power, but alas not consistency. Bedi left it to Madan Lal and Rakesh Shukla to do most of the damage, and came on only to bowl at the left-hander K. Balaji, fresh from resounding success at the university level and with a century on debut in the previous Ranji match. (Other famous bowlers, for example Freddie Trueman, were known to bowl in a similar situation only to knock down an aspiring youngster a peg or two, but the absent-minded Sardar most likely wasn't aware of Balaji's recent feats—he probably just felt like bowling to a left-hander.) After playing and missing most of one over, Balaji came crashing down the wicket to hit Bedi over the top, missed, but so did the portly wicket-keeper, Inderjit Singh, and the ball went for four byes. Bedi immediately pulled Surinder Amarnath—unlike his brother, a brilliant fielder—out of the off-side, and with his spikes marked out a spot at very straight and short mid-on, no more than three or four paces from the bowler. Mesmerized, Balaji played the next ball off the meat of his bat—as if giving fielding practice— and Surinder stooped low to pick up the catch. My most enduring memory, however, is of poor Balaji fielding late in the day under the Willingdon Pavilion—a forlorn figure, his three sweaters inadequate protection against the advancing Delhi winter and the magic of Bishen Singh Bedi.

There will be only one Bedi, and with his departure the art and craft of left-arm spin has gone into a precipitous decline. It is well known that his powers of turn and deceptive flight marked him out from the run of international bowlers. It is less well recognized that his control was immaculate. If by a bad ball is meant one directed away from the stumps, or short pitched, or a full toss, I can honestly say that in dozens of hours of watching Bedi I never once saw him bowl a bad ball. Certainly he was hit for fours and sixes, but only when the batsman came down the wicket to convert a good length delivery into a half volley or full pitch (I can't recall Bedi being cut, though I do remember England's Barry Wood bowled attempting the stroke). Wilfred Rhodes, who is Bedi's only real rival for the title of being the greatest slow left-armer in the history of the game, once commented on his successor in the Yorkshire side, the marginally inferior Hedley Verity: 'I see he has one delivery which I never could master—the one slightly short of a length which the batsman pushes past square leg for a single'. Bedi could likewise say, with justice, of Doshi, Maninder and Shastri— and no disrespect meant to those fine cricketers and competitors—'I see they all have one delivery I never did possess—the half volley outside the leg stump which the batsman sweeps for four'.

1. *The Sardar of Spin* 2. *Lala da Laadla (Lala's favourite son)*
3. *'Six to Win!', says the opener from Poona*

VI

Three places remain to be filled, and a host of university stars to consider. Candidates for the remaining middle order spot include Manmohan Sood—in his only Test he was unlucky to come up against Alan Davidson in his prime—and Prem Bhatia and Gulshan Rai, both attacking strokeplayers who hovered around the national side. Nor can one forget the graceful Ramesh Saxena, who made his mark as a Delhi schoolboy before moving east to Bihar. A marvellous player of spin bowling, Saxena too played only one Test, at Lord's in 1967. There, with one of those errors of judgement in which Indian cricket abounds, he was asked to open the innings.

For all its varied bowling talents, Delhi cricket has not been well served by wicket-keepers. The only stumper of international quality to play for Delhi was K.S. Indrajitsinhji, in his years at St Stephen's College. However, Indrajit played for Saurashtra both before and after he lived in the capital, and as he was coached at Ranji's Jamnagar palace, he must be reserved for a later chapter. As I write, young Mohan Chaturvedi is on the fringes of the Indian side, but pending his advancement we must choose Surinder Khanna, the hard-hitting batsman from Hindu College who kept wickets for India in the 1979 World Cup.

As for the all-rounder's place, it is a toss-up between two more Hindu College stalwarts, Prakash Bhandari (off-spin) and Rakesh Shukla (leg break but mostly googly). With two left-arm spinners in the side, Bhandari may just sneak in for variety. Readers may note the unswerving impartiality with which I have gone about the task; a Stephanian cricketer myself, I have chosen no fewer than three Hindu College players and not one from my own college.

66

VII

An all-time Delhi eleven, composed almost equally of university stars and migrants from the Punjab, is offered below. But if you want to replace Saxena with Sood, or Lamba with Akash Lal—as I nearly did myself in the proofs of this book—I shall not mind in the least.

1. C.P.S. Chauhan
2. R. Lamba
3. S. Amarnath
4. M. Amarnath
5. R. Saxena
6. P. Bhandari
7. S. Madan Lal
8. S. Khanna (wicket-keeper)
9. R. Pal
10. B.S. Bedi (captain)
11. R. Goel
12th man: Maninder Singh

With the magnificent exception of Chetan Pratap Singh Chauhan, this then is an all-Punjabi XI, a befitting tribute to the enterprise and resourcefulness of the city's leading community. And with the exception of perhaps the most modest cricketer who ever lived, Rajinder Goel, all have captained Delhi at one time or another. But there is no dispute about who is in charge here. Bedi early on acquired the sobriquet of 'Paaji' [Elder Brother], both as a mark of respect and to distinguish him from the eminence grise of Delhi cricket, Ram Prakash Mehra 'Shahji' [Honoured Sir]. While the seemingly indestructible Shahji passed away a few years ago, Paaji will hopefully be with us for some time yet. Meanwhile, let us celebrate him not only as cricketer but as human being. Pataudi once said of Bedi that 'he is the only cricketer of my acquaintance who spends more money on others than others spend on him'. In these post-Packer days, this is surely one of the most sincere tributes one cricketer can pay another.

CHAPTER FOUR

Nawabs and Commoners
in Hyderabad

*J*f Athens and Sparta were the two great city-states
of ancient Greece, then Hyderabad and Bombay
are surely the two champion cities of Indian
cricket. Far stronger in cricketing terms than the
states of which they are part—Andhra Pradesh and
Maharashtra—they have supplied a steady stream of players
for the Test team. Admittedly, they are not the only teams to
play as cities in the Ranji Trophy. There is a third, Baroda, but
despite the Gaekwads, father and son, J.M. Ghorpade, Kiran
More, and of course the incomparable Hazare, it isn't quite in
the same league. A fourth, Delhi, has been considered sepa-
rately, but its rise is relatively recent—in cricketing terms it is
nouveau riche.

The Grecian analogy can be stretched still further. Just as
Athens and Sparta were split in two halves, a free born democratic portion and a slave section, respectively, so too Bombay
and Hyderabad have each had two very distinct cricketing
mileux. In Chapter Two, we have already noted the island city's
two cricketing cultures. Similarly, it has always seemed to me
that the social geography of Hyderabad is perfectly mirrored
in the contrasting cricketing styles of its most famous players.
The spacious palaces of the aristocratic elite have generated

69

one cricketing ethos, the narrow lanes and small houses of the old city yet another.

Again, Hyderabad and Bombay are the only Indian cities to have hosted cricket tournaments that are recognized as 'first class'. The Bombay Pentangular has long since passed into history, but Hyderabad's own tournament—named for a nawab, of course—is yet played when the domestic calendar allows. Endowed by Nawab Moin-ud-Dowlah, who watched the early matches from his Rolls Royce, it was later taken over by the Hyderabad Cricket Association (HCA). This is very likely the only cricket tournament in the world where teams and individuals can play by invitation only. That is, cricketers cannot simply wish to play in the tournament, nor can teams qualify through competition—they have to be invited by the HCA through its moving spirit, P.R. Man Singh. Hyderabad does not often get to host a Test match, but the Moin-ud-Dowlah Gold Cup has, year after year, brought the city the finest cricketing talent in India, as well as elsewhere—for the great English opening pair of Hobbs and Sutcliffe appeared for the Maharajkumar of Vizianagaram's XI in the first year of the Cup, while Learie Constantine and Rohan Kanhai have graced the occasion since.

II

Moin-ud-Dowlah was not, however, a prince who played. On the field, the 'nawabi' style in Hyderabad cricket was exemplified by the Nawab himself, Mansur Ali Khan of Pataudi, who abandoned Delhi for Hyderabad, and by his fellow Oxonian Abbas Ali Baig. Just to prove that class distinctions cut across religious boundaries, it must also include the city's most famous captain, Motganahalli Laxminarasu Jaisimha. While these three have been the great nawabs of Hyderabad cricket, lesser noblemen who have played for the city's Ranji Trophy team include the Cambridge Blue Santosh Reddy, and Abbas's younger brother Murtaza Ali Baig, who was an Oxford Blue.

'Tiger', 'Buggy' and 'Jai' were as dashing a trio of lady killers as ever trod a cricket field. With sleeves buttoned to the wrist, perfectly creased cream trousers, and silk chokers, they were living testimony of the adage, 'the apparel oft proclaims the man' (and need we add, batsman). Although Tiger and Jai were far better known for their often fatal effect on the fairer sex, Buggy was no slouch in this respect, once evoking open adulation in the form of the lady who ran on to the field to kiss him for completing fifty in a Bombay Test. The trio's favourite strokes were indeed the regal ones—the cut, hook and cover drive. Jai once so far forgot himself as to bat all five days of a Test—setting a world record in the process—and Tiger was known to potter around in his last days as an international player, but in the main the nawabs' batting styles bore the unmistakable stamp of their social origins.

The aristocratic lineage of the nawabs of Hyderabad cricket is manifest, too, in the almost dream-like entry which Abbas Ali Baig made into Test cricket. A freshman at Oxford in 1959, Baig was preparing to join the Somerset County Cricket Club at the culmination of the University season, when an Indian touring side badly hit by injuries called upon his services. He had been prepared for that call by a strong campaign in the press, led by Keith Miller, which pleaded: 'Don't be vague, ask for Baig!' Using that caption, a cartoon of the time showed a miniature Baig, playing his favourite square cut, inside a [Haig] whisky bottle carrying the label, 'Oxford vintage'.

Joining a demoralized team already three down in the series, Buggy lifted its spirits somewhat with a crisp 46 in the first innings of the Manchester Test. He did even better the second time around, hitting a strokeful hundred and, in association with the veteran Umrigar, nearly saved the game for India. Although India lost the last Test as well, Baig's brilliance had provided a brief flicker of light in an otherwise unremittingly grim summer.

If Buggy made a fairy-tale entrance into Test cricket, Jaisimha is perhaps best known for his fairy-tale comeback. Again, this was for a touring side crippled by injuries, in Australia in 1968. Asked to name a replacement, Pataudi called for his old Hyderabad colleague. Twenty-four hours after stepping off the plane, Jai was playing in the Third Test at the Brisbane cricket ground. Astonishingly, he found his touch without so much as a practice net, and scored 74 and 101 not out in the match. The latter innings carried India to within thirty-nine runs of what would have been its first win on Australian soil. Jai had done what was humanly possible, but it was not enough. There is, somewhere, a moving picture of Jai walking off the Gabba at the end of the match. The Australian team and the Indian number eleven are already in the pavilion, but a dazed Jai, handsome as ever and with his collar turned up in his inimitable style, is walking slowly and disbelievingly off the ground, surrounded by a group of admiring schoolboys.

As for Tiger Pataudi, he made both a fairy-tale entry and several fairy-tale comebacks to big cricket. He was a prodigy at the English public school of Winchester, where he broke D.R. Jardine's record aggregate for the school season. This was justice of a kind, for Jardine and Pataudi's father had had a famous row in the Bodyline series. After scoring a cultured hundred in the first Test of that series, the senior Pataudi was dropped after failing with the bat in the next match, in part because as a 'conscientious objector' he refused to field in the leg trap Jardine had set for Harold Larwood.

The younger Pataudi's batting at Winchester encouraged

his cricket master, the former England player Hubert Doggart, to recommend him to the Sussex county side. Pataudi then made his first-class debut, at sixteen, for a team for which both Ranji and Duleep had played (like the princes of Nawanagar, Pataudi was to captain Sussex in due course). Proceeding to Oxford in 1960, he emulated his father by hitting a century in the Varsity match against Cambridge. Appointed captain of Oxford the next season, he hit two stunning hundreds against a strong Yorkshire side. (The nawabs of Hyderabad seemed to relish the Yorkshire bowling. In the previous year, Abbas Ali Baig, in an innings of 150 against the Champion county, square cut Ray Illingworth so masterfully that he had the off-spinner bowl to him with a third man and cover point on the boundary—and this on a turning wicket).

With three matches left to play in 1961, Pataudi needed just 92 runs to overhaul his father's record for the most runs scored in an Oxford season. But just as Tiger seemed poised for greatness, he met with a serious automobile accident, after which he lost sight in one eye. Remarkably, he learnt to bat with this handicap, and in a year's time was playing for India. Shortly afterwards, he became the youngest ever Test captain—at twenty-one—when Nari Contractor was felled by Charlie Griffith in Barbados. He then embarked on a long stint as captain— marked by some notable successes including India's first Test and series wins abroad. For a decade Pataudi, despite his cruel handicap, was also India's best batsman, next only to Chandu Borde. Among a host of courageous innings, two stunning performances in England and Australia earned him the title of the Nawab of Headingley and Melbourne. When his batting form temporarily deserted him, Pataudi was replaced as captain of India and omitted for the 1971 tour of the West Indies. When Wadekar's side were successful in both the West Indies and England, most people were ready to write Pataudi off. But not Tiger himself. He worked his way back into the side for the home series against England, where he hit two fine fifties, though he probably considers his 14 not out in the Madras Test, made when India lost six wickets reaching a target of 92, to be one of his most valuable Test knocks (it was indeed a little gem of an innings). After opting out of the England tour of 1974, Pat was back once more the next winter, to lead India in the thrilling series against Clive Lloyd's team.

III

These then are the chronicles, briefly told, of the nawabs of Hyderabad cricket. The city's commoners, for their part, found their cricketing hero in that sturdy all-rounder Syed Abid Ali, who hit the winning stroke in the epic Oval Test of 1971. Abid, who had never seen a Test match till he played in one, was known locally as 'Chicha' (father's younger brother), an avuncular epithet no one dare use on any of the lordly trio. Although he now makes his living coaching in, of all places, the United States, Abid never played an orthodox stroke in his life. Far more revealing was his bowling style. Where other fast bowlers have their slower one, Abid put great store by his lower one, a lethal delivery well known as the *surrrah* to anyone who has ever played *gully* (street) cricket. Abid's most famous *surrrah* was the one that got rid of Roy Fredericks first ball in the 1971 Port of Spain Test in which India beat the West Indies for the first time (for the startled Fredericks, wrote Raju Bharatan, it was a case of 'being hit below the boot'). Ironically, Abid started bowling quite late in his first-class career. He began as a wicket-keeper for the State Bank of India (he even kept wickets for India in a Test match, when Engineer was injured). Capped by Hyderabad as a batsman in the late nineteen-fifties, he occasionally kept wickets for the state. It was only when

Hyderabad's regular stumper, R. Venkatesh, joined the State Bank that Abid took to bowling. By 1965 he was opening the bowling for Hyderabad, and two years later for India.

It was indeed as a bowler and fielder that Abid contributed most to Wadekar's side of the early seventies, though he did play some fine attacking innings late in the order. On his first Australian tour, where he opened the innings, no less a person than Jack Fingleton remarked that 'Abid Ali has it within himself to become a great batsman'. Although I have watched him in the flesh many times, it is a sight of him in a film of the Oval Test that sticks in the mind. At his own—and Indian cricket's—greatest moment, Abid hit the winning square cut off Brian Luckhurst, and turned for the pavilion. As he did, he saw Alan Knott and Keith Fletcher rush to grab the stumps at his end. Abid turned around, and seeing that the wickets at the bowler's end were still intact, decided that he too wanted a souvenir. Running like a terrier for his prize, he was met by the umpire, arms outstretched, while behind the umpire was an advancing crowd of delirious Indians. The film cuts at this point, but I am willing to have a small wager—a packet of Charminar cigarettes perhaps—that Abid caught his souvenir—in the end.

Another equally distinguished representative of the commoner grain of Hyderabad culture is one who is in cricketing terms Abid's nephew, Mohammed Azharuddin. Like Abid, Azhar was educated at the city's All Saints School, but, like Abid again, he clearly learnt his cricket outside the school premises. The cover drive is reputed to be the most classical shot in the game, yet I have seen Azhar, more than once, manage the remarkable feat of playing it, *with a horizontal bat,* from well outside the leg stump. But of course the straight bat is a positive liability in the gullies, whose bumps, holes, and angles make the Lord's pitch, with its famous ridge, look and play like a billiards table in comparison.

I have already spoken of Abid's versatility; like Lala Amarnath, he was a wicket-keeper who became in time the country's leading new ball bowler. Brought up in a lower-middle-class family, Azhar too has had to fashion a veritable tool kit of survival skills. He is, of course, quite outstanding in the field. A specialist at cover, in one day matches Azhar was normally stationed by his Hyderabad colleague, Arshad Ayub, at deep square leg, for the off-spinner—as miserly as they come—could not trust anyone else to handle the wicked flight and bounce of a firmly swept ball. Thrust into the slips in a Test in Pakistan, Azhar equalled a world record with five catches in an innings. While in the side primarily as a batsman, at a pinch Azhar has also bowled off breaks in the one day game. The semi-final of the Nehru Cup of 1989 even saw Azhar bowl leg breaks—his original style—as Srikkanth tried desperately to make inroads into the West Indies batting. And no doubt before his career is over Azhar shall emulate Abid Ali by keeping wickets in a Test match.

If the angle of their bat sets Abid and Azhar apart from the nawabs, their fielding style is equally unorthodox. Here, Azhar has taken Pataudi's place as the finest cover point in the game. But while the Nawab, as befitting a product of Winchester and Oxford, fielded in the classical style, with his right leg a full yard behind the left one, Azhar has relied more on his ability to jerk sideways and grab the ball. But whatever the coaches might say, the marvellously inventive styles and combative spirits of Abid and Azhar have stood their city and country in good stead. If one had to pick a man to bat, or indeed field, for one's life, the two commoners would be far better choices than any of the three nawabs of Hyderabad cricket.

1 & 2. The commoners 3 & 4. The nawabs (apologies to that nawab and gentleman, Abbas Ali Baig)

IV

While Azhar belongs to a later generation, I did once see the three nawabs and Abid in action together. In Bombay to participate in an inter-college quiz in the spring of 1976, I gladly gave the quiz a miss and made my way to the newly built Wankhede Stadium to watch Hyderabad play Bombay. Hyderabad were batting, and we were treated to a crisp opening stand between Baig and K. Jayantilal, a fine opening bat unlucky to be around the same age as Gavaskar. The great disappointments were Pataudi and Jaisimha, by then batting from memory. But that simply wasn't good enough against Shivalkar and an incredibly youthful Sandeep Patil, making his Ranji Trophy debut as a medium pacer on the strength of some outstanding performances at the university level. Hyderabad's pride was salvaged somewhat by Abid, who hit Shivalkar several times over mid-wicket in a brief stay, and a late rally by the wicket-keeper Vijay Paul and Sultan Saleem, the last named a schoolboy prodigy who never quite fulfilled his early promise.

Notwithstanding the distinctions of class and culture, it must be said that in this case opposites unite to form a remarkably effective whole. Any side would be happy with a batting side whose first six would be the three nawabs, the two commoners, and E.B. Aibara. Later a renowned coach, the bespectacled Aibara held the Hyderabad batting together for the first two decades. Invariably sporting a multi-coloured cap, he was an orthodox batsman, who, as befitting a coach, always knew exactly where his off stump was. The first time Hyderabad won the Ranji Trophy, in 1938-9, Aibara played a match-winning innings of 137 not out in a one-wicket victory over Amar Singh's Nawanagar. Here, Aibara would edge out both Jayantilal and the Davis Cup star S.M. Hadi, who scored the first ever hundred in the Ranji Trophy.

V

As for the bowling, the first name that comes to mind is of an off-spinner of enormous skill who suffered greatly from the uncertain catching of his close fielders. Ghulam Ahmed won some consolation when he ended up as a top cricket administrator, but he surely deserved more than his 68 Test wickets. Better fielding—perhaps the likes of Abid and Azhar—would have made Mankad, Gupte and Ghulam as effective as Bedi, Chandrasekhar and Prasanna, who could count on the services of such fine catchers as Wadekar, Solkar, Venkat, and Abid himself.

Ghulam was capped rather late for India (nearly ten years after his first class debut), most likely because the Hyderabad Ranji Trophy team, which relied heavily on one batsman, Aibara, and one bowler, himself, very rarely got past the second round of what was then a purely knock-out competition. He was also, erroneously, believed to be a matting wicket bowler. But on the Chepauk turf in 1945, Ghulam nearly bowled South Zone to a famous victory over the Australian Services side. His eight victims in that match included the wicket in each innings of Keith Miller, both times for low scores (0 and 8). That fine student of the game, C.P. Johnstone of Madras, was fielding at slip, but despite Johnstone's urgings Ghulam was not chosen for the 1946 tour of England. He should certainly have gone on that tour—instead of one of the two leg-spinners who were selected—when he would have been a perfect foil in a wet summer to Vinoo Mankad.

K.N. Prabhu recently wrote that, as a bowler, Ghulam 'combined the best of Prasanna and Venkataraghavan'. To others like myself who never saw him bowl, this must seem an extraordinary claim. But to Prabhu's claim I can add the testimony of Ghulam's fellow off-spinner, V.M. Muddiah.

79

Ghulam kept Muddiah, and some other first-rate off-spinners out of the Indian side for nearly a decade; but despite (or perhaps because of) this, the latter's admiration for the Hyderabad wizard was unbounded. Well after Ghulam had retired, Muddiah accompanied a Bangalore club side on a cricket tour of Hyderabad. As the cricketers sat talking in the Fateh Maidan pavilion after the day's play, Muddiah suddenly exclaimed: 'There comes the world's greatest bowler'. In walked Ghulam, erect as ever, and Muddiah persuaded him to put on a little show. By now Ghulam was well into his fifties, and had not played competitive cricket for over a decade. Nonetheless, he had three stumps placed on the wicket and, in civilian clothes, went on his run. His first ball hit the off stump, the second the middle stump, and the third the leg stump.

On an earlier occasion, Muddiah was the non-striker in a match played on the mat, when Ghulam came on to bowl. Like Mankad and Bedi, Ghulam invariably dropped on a length straightaway, but this time his first ball was short and comfortably pulled round to square leg. 'I don't know what's wrong', remarked Ghulam to Muddiah. Surprisingly, the second ball too was quite short. 'I can't remember when I bowled two in a row like this', said Ghulam. When the third ball too pitched short, Ghulam insisted the match be stopped. He called for the groundsman, who measured the mat and, sure enough, discovered it was eighteen inches too long.

Picking partners for Ghulam is an unenviable task. Other outstanding Hyderabad off-spinners include a Parsi, Nausher Mehta, a Tamil, V. Ramnarayan, a Sikh, Kanwaljit Singh, and a Muslim, Arshad Ayub (not to speak of the many-sided Jaisimha). I personally fancy Ayub's close contemporary and immediate predecessor in the Indian team, Shivlal Yadav. Shivlal, whose powers of flight and spin were at times not unworthy of Prasanna, had his confidence badly shattered by

80

Gavaskar's faith in medium pace and penchant for slowing the game down. Even so, he played long and well enough to capture more than a one hundred wickets in Test cricket. Like Ghulam (not to speak of Lance Gibbs, Jim Laker and Prasanna!) Shivlal always bowled particularly well against the Australians.

The third spinner's slot must clearly be filled by someone who breaks from leg to off. One possibility is Mumtaz Hussain, who bowled both orthodox left-arm and back-of-the-hand stuff. Another is Venkatapathy Raju, the recent Test cap who is one of the few Hyderabad cricketers whose home is not in the city but in the Andhra Pradesh heartland. A third is the all-rounder M.V. Narasimha Rao, the poor man's Chandrasekhar whose flowing locks were rudely chopped when he went to Tirupati on being at last selected for India. (In shaving his head at the holiest of holies, he was only anticipating N.T. Rama Rao, who did the same thing on being elected Chief Minister of Andhra Pradesh.)

VI

That leaves just two places to be filled. One is that of the wicket keeper, and despite the dash of the university star A.A.S. Asif (the first-choice keeper for Indian Schoolboys in the late sixties, when Syed Kirmani played for the team as a batsman) we must plump for the only international stumper from Hyderabad, P. Krishnamurthy. Safe rather than spectacular, Krishnamurthy did a fine job when Engineer was barred from selection, on account of his refusal to play domestic cricket, for the West Indies tour of 1971.

I have left the juiciest morsel for the last. Fair cheating is allowed in playing favourites. And for the eleventh spot we can just sneak in a man who made his fame and fortune playing for another state, Kent, and another country, Pakistan, but who began life in the Charminar city. Yes, Ghulam Ahmed's nephew Asif Iqbal did play as a seventeen-year-old for Hyderabad before migrating across the border. What a wonderful foil he would make for Abid! The mind boggles at the thought. Quick as terriers between the wickets, electrifying fieldsmen, handy seam bowlers, and unorthodox but highly effective batsmen, the two have a great deal in common—though it must be said that Asif was just that bit better in all departments. If our cheating is permitted by the hideously rule bound mandarins of the Board of Control for Cricket in India, Asif would provide the perfect finishing touch—the commoner who played like a prince.

VII

This is our all-time Hyderabad eleven, perhaps less controversial than most.

1. M.L. Jaisimha (captain)
2. A.A. Baig
3. M.A.K. Pataudi
4. E.B. Aibara
5. Md Azharuddin
6. Asif Iqbal
7. S. Abid Ali
8. P. Krishnamurthy (wicket-keeper)
9. N.S. Yadav
10. Mumtaz Hussain
11. Ghulam Ahmed
12th man : K. Jayantilal

Although Jaisimha himself would never countenance the suggestion, he must be chosen captain ahead of Ghulam

Ahmed. Successive Indian skippers acknowledged his immense tactical skills—Pataudi by playing under him for Hyderabad, Wadekar by having him as twelfth man, to give advice, when Jai's batting form deserted him on his last overseas tour in the West Indies in 1971. Only Aibara comes close to his record of service. Jai played twenty-three seasons for Hyderabad, at least fifteen as captain. Sadly, Hyderabad never won the Ranji Trophy during Jai's playing career, though his son, Vivek, was a member of the winning side of 1986–7.

CHAPTER FIVE

Majestic Mysore

*I*n 1966 I made what turned out to be an incredibly shrewd decision for an eight-year-old. This was the year the sporting bug first hit me, the last page of the newspaper just beginning to make sense. My first aural memories are of the historic World Cup soccer final of 1966, in which England beat West Germany in extra time, and of Colin Milburn's heroic counter-attack against Gary Sobers's all conquering West Indians, both carried live into the drawing room by the BBC. On the domestic front, I had to take the momentous step of choosing a Ranji Trophy side to support: a decision whose consequences I would have to consider very carefully indeed, for I could be stuck with it for a lifetime.

There were really only three options: the state I grew up in, Uttar Pradesh; the state my ancestors came from, Tamil Nadu; and the state where my grandparents had recently moved, Karnataka (then Mysore). U.P. ruled itself out for obvious reasons—at the time it was the weakest team in the weakest zone—so the choice was between the two southern giants. My final decision was made easy by the presence, in the Indian team then playing the West Indies, of no less than three cricketers from Mysore (Prasanna, Chandrasekhar and the state captain, V. Subrahmanyam)—that too, in the Madras Test, a match India would have won but for an improbable ninth-wicket stand between Sobers and, of all people, Charlie Griffith.

Within a decade, my choice had begun to pay dividends. For it fell to Karnataka, in a match of which I watched every ball, to break Bombay's interminably long reign as Ranji champions, and by 1983 they had won the championship no less than three times. More importantly, by breaking Bombay's stranglehold, my team contributed to a significant decentring of Indian cricket, opening the way for other teams like Delhi, Hyderabad (and yes, Tamil Nadu) to win the trophy in later years.

II

Karnataka's meteoric rise in Indian cricket centred around the performances of four maestros, all of whom figure in my all-time Indian XI and who would have walked into most contemporary World XI's in their prime—E.A.S. Prasanna, B.S. Chandrasekhar, G.R. Viswanath and S.M.H. Kirmani. Yet, as Prasanna handsomely acknowledges in his autobiography, the foundation for Mysore's success had been laid by his predecessor as captain, V. Subrahmanyam. 'Subbu' showed only glimpses of his attacking strokeplay and prehensile catching in the nine Tests he played—a fifty in Madras against the West Indies in 1966–7, a blazing 75 (run out) in the Adelaide Test the following winter—but he was an inspiring leader under whose tutelage at least three of the four maestros took their first steps in first-class cricket.

Subbu's successor as captain of Mysore was arguably the most intelligent spin bowler who ever lived. I was twelve when I first saw Prasanna in action, leading City Cricketers against the Indian Air Force in Bangalore's Y.S. Ramaswamy tournament. The Air Force side had one star batsman, D.D. Deshpande, who played with distinction for four states and two zones and also figures in *Wisden* as one of the few cricketers to be given out obstructing the field in a first-class match. At one end the leg boundary was very short—barely forty yards—and the crafty Prasanna came on to bowl at that very boundary. In each of his first two overs, he bowled one off-break fractionally short of a length, both of which the alert Deshpande despatched first bounce into the adjoining Cubbon Park (for those who are familiar with Bangalore, this was the Y.M.C.A ground). Having set the batsman up, in his third over 'Pras' sent down what looked like an identical ball—only this time it did not turn and hurried through off the wicket, catching Deshpande leg-before. Having disposed of the main threat, Pras retired from the fray, leaving the pickings to his young proteges, the off-spinner Prasanna Narasimha Rao and the left-armer B. Vijaykrishna. (Chandrasekhar, who also played for City Cricketers, didn't even get to bowl.)

Much later, I read a similar story about the master bowler, S.F. Barnes. Bowling to the formidable Albert Hollowood in the Staffordshire league, Barnes fed him two off-side long hops, which predictably went whistling past point's left hand for four. 'You don't bowl short to Albert', expostulated Barnes's captain, 'its four every time'. Barnes merely nodded, and in the next over bowled a seemingly identical ball which this time broke back sharply and trapped Hollowood leg-before. Barnes ran triumphantly to his skipper: 'Two into four makes eight. Albert usually gets fifty'.

But to return to Bangalore and the summer of 1970. In the next round of the Y.S.R. tournament, City Cricketers were to meet the Crescents Cricket Club. Crescents had a big hitter named Venugopal who had been bragging about what he would do to Prasanna when they met. Word got around of

Venugopal's challenge, and a fair crowd came to watch the clash at the Railway Institute ground, abutting the Bangalore City Railway Station. When 'Venu' walked in to face Prasanna, the bowler had deliberately left a huge gap at mid-on. Venu, whose bat bore the Indian hitter's distinctive stamp, a three-inch-wide white tape across its lower end, had only two strokes, a forward defensive lunge and the lofted drive, which he normally played by turn. After Two-Stroke Venu had hit him for one towering six on to the railway tracks, Pras pulled Chandrasekhar out of the off-side and sent him to the long-on boundary. Venu ritually prodded forward to the next ball, and then the off-spinner threw one up—only it was not quite there for the big hit. Chandrasekhar, always a safe field, accepted the skier, and Pras had made yet another batsman eat his words.

Two-Stroke Venu I never saw again. But years later I played against D.D. Deshpande. At lunch I approached him with the story of where I had first seen him bat. No sooner had I begun than he exclaimed, 'Ah yes, Pras. He made a fool of me that day'. But where Prasanna enticed batsmen to their doom, his bowling partner for club, state, zone and country, Bhagawat Chandrasekhar, positively hustled them out. This is not to say that the received wisdom, that 'Chandra' was an instinctive rather than thinking bowler, has even a grain of truth. I well remember a group of us going to watch our college mate Arun Lal make his Ranji Trophy debut for Delhi against Karnataka, at the Kotla in the winter of 1974. Arun's first ball in first-class cricket was Chandra's famous fast googly—pitched in close on the off stump, it spun back—in the phrase of a long forgotten sports writer—like a King Cobra with a hangover. Arun managed to nick it on to his pad, from where it rebounded to Sanjay Desai at short-leg. Having softened up his prey, Chandra now threw up a lovely flighted leg-break. As Arun made to drive, the ball swerved in ever so slightly, eluded his bat, and spun a good six inches to take the off bail.

Four years later, and on the same ground, I watched Chandra's last triumph in big cricket, five wickets for a hundred odd on a slow wicket against one of the most powerful batting sides in the country. The left-handers Venkat Sunderam and Surinder Amarnath, both fine players of spin bowling, were beaten on the back foot by Chandra's leg-break, which spun quickly enough on a dead Kotla wicket to catch them leg-before. I remember Madan Lal, who hit a battling hundred, being mesmerized in one Chandra over—he was beaten four times in a row, and then the extra bounce of a leg-break surprised him into edging a catch to slip's right hand, which the bulky Viswanath reached but just failed to hold. At the end of the over Madan reclined on his bat, a look of sheer wonder on his face—after years of playing with and against Chandra, he still couldn't fathom the googly bowler.

For me, Arun Lal's first two deliveries in the Ranji Trophy had given the lie to the joke—one doing the rounds ever since Chandrasekhar made his Test debut as an eighteen-year-old against Mike Smith's Englishmen—that if the bowler did not know what he was bowling, how could the batsman? Rajan Bala was so angered by this canard that he once said that whoever first spread it should be put in 'a miserably cold cell in Tihar [jail] with Pathan warders cracking whips all over where it hurts'. I doubt whether the gentle Chandra would wish such a fate on anybody, but he did work hard and knowingly at his craft. Essentially a googly bowler, Chandra's leg-break was perfectly disguised, while his many caught-and-bowled victims are testimony to the subtlety of his flight. Two of the six batsmen he dismissed while winning the Oval Test in 1971 were in fact out in this manner, one of whom was the canny Yorkshireman Ray Illingworth, deceived by a dipping leg-break into hitting the ball early and in the air back to the bowler.

I once heard Conrad Hunte unwittingly pay a remarkable tribute to Chandrasekhar. In a talk in Delhi long after he had left cricket for Moral Rearmament, the West Indian opener was describing how, on the Indian tour of 1966-7, Gary Sobers had asked him, as the batsman with the impeccable technique, to take on Chandra. Hunte explained at length how he batted with his left hand very loose on the handle, so that even if he misread Chandra's turn, the edge would not carry to short leg if it was a googly, or to slip, if it was the leg-break. (Conrad, like his team-mates, couldn't read the wrist-spinner from the hand.) By these methods Hunte batted six and a half hours for 107 in the Calcutta Test, laying the platform for a match-winning total. Even as Hunte finished a story which he intended to reflect well solely on himself, a voice in the audience mischievously interjected: 'Mr. Hunte, perhaps it was Chandra who won in the end'. 'How so', enquired a puzzled Hunte. 'If you, a West Indian, took as many as six and a half hours to score a mere 107, surely the victory was Chandra's', came the reply. Hunte threw his head back, and laughing delightedly, agreed.

III

Sunil Gavaskar once wrote that the most terrifying sound in Test cricket—for the visiting batsman, at any rate—was a crowd of 80,000 at the Eden Gardens in Calcutta shouting 'bo..o..wled' as Chandra ran up to bowl. Perhaps, but by the same token the most joyous sound in cricket was the same crowd cheering when Chandra, while batting, actually managed to play the ball. For Chandra was indisputably one of the two most popular cricketers to have played for India, the other being his team-mate and close friend Gundappa Viswanath.

At this point I must declare an interest. Viswanath was the first Test cricketer I ever shook hands with, in the same summer of 1970 when I first saw Prasanna and Chandrasekhar playing in the Y.S.R. tournament. This was barely a few months after Viswanath's dazzling entry into Test cricket against Bill Lawry's Australians. He had been included in the Kanpur Test only at the insistence of the captain, Pataudi, and when he scored a duck in the first innings, his head was on the chopping block. But, as everyone knows, Viswanath scored a match-saving century the second time around, 137 not out with no less than twenty-five boundaries. He followed this innings with a share in the match-winning stand with Ajit Wadekar in Delhi, and two fifties in the last Test at Madras which India lost, but barely. When I met him, therefore, 'Vishy' was savouring the first months of his entry into the big time. It had not yet sunk in that as a centurion on debut he was tempting fate: for all previous Indians who had made a hundred in their first Test—Lala Amarnath, Deepak Shodhan, Kripal Singh, Abbas Ali Baig and Hanumant Singh—failed to reach three figures again. Viswanath was to break the sequence with his hundred against England in Bombay in 1973, thus paving the way for Azharuddin's run of three centuries in his first three Tests. (In between, another debut centurion, Surinder Amarnath, had like his father succumbed to the jinx.)

Eighteen years, or half a lifetime, after I first shook hands with him, I watched Viswanath score a hundred for his employer, the State Bank of India, in the semi-finals of a Bangalore tournament. When I reached the ground (KSCA 'matting', adjoining the scene of some of Viswanath's greatest triumphs, the Chinnaswamy Stadium) he was batting with his long-time colleague for club, state and country, Syed Kirmani. On this day, Vishy was content to push and deflect for singles so long as 'Kiri' was there, rotating the strike to the advantage of the hard-hitting wicket-keeper batsman. When Kiri left—characteristically, caught at long on—Vishy took over. Striking three successive sixes off the opposing slow-left-armer—straight, over long-off and over extra-cover—he was within striking distance of his hundred. In this limited-overs match, the side batting first had to close at noon, and at ten minutes to twelve Vishy was 89. On hand was a crowd of perhaps 300 people: as many as would today watch Karnataka in a Ranji Trophy match, and I bet on this occasion all but a few were there, like myself, only on the slim chance that Vishy would be in good nick. A leg-side deflection and the famous square cut took him to 95. Then, running a sharp two to cover he was struck a painful blow on his toe, as he came in the way of a crisp return to the wicket-keeper. Immediately, all the fielders rushed to him, for hurting the most loved man in cricket has always caused more pain to the fielder or bowler concerned than to Vishy himself. In any case, the fielding side were as keen as we were that he reach what had become for him an elusive milestone in any class of cricket. Thankfully, Vishy was not seriously hurt, and completed his century at the dot of twelve. As he did, one of his admirers rushed on to the ground to realize the dreams of a lifetime—something he was no doubt emboldened to do by the absence of the barriers, both material and physical, that he would have encountered in a Test match. Where other Test cricketers would have expressed annoyance and waved the intruder away, Vishy shook his hand (thereby placing the latter in the same league as myself, for surely Vishy was the first Test cricketer *he* had shaken hands with), and with a word of thanks sent him on his way.

Vishy's courtesy to that admirer was characteristic of the man. For in his chosen trade, Viswanath has always adhered to the most noble values without once having to proclaim it from the rooftops. Throughout his long career, and even when he was out of form, Vishy was one of the very few 'walkers' among Test batsmen. The most celebrated example of his innate generosity was of course the decision in only his second, and as it happened, last Test as captain, to recall the England wicket-keeper Bob Taylor when he had been wrongly given out in the Jubilee Test of 1980—an act which probably cost India the match. Bob Willis wrote of that incident: 'Viswanath's action recalled that of [Australia's] Rod Marsh in the Centenary Test three years earlier, when he recalled [England's] Derek Randall. That gesture by Marsh came as a bit of a shock, and it is indicative of the respect England's players have for Viswanath that his intervention seemed wholly typical.'

Vishy's character was so transparently true that it unbent even his most dour opponents. His last great innings was a hundred he scored in the low-scoring Melbourne Test of 1981, which India won by barely fifty runs. When Vishy was finally out, the Australian side rose to him. As he passed the slips on his way to the pavilion, the fielding team's captain, Greg Chappell, smiling warmly all the while, tapped Vishy affectionately on the head. I don't believe the man who directed the notorious underarm incident was given to such open commendation of an opponent (thus I cannot see Chappell doing the same thing to Viv Richards or Geoff Boycott), but Vishy had this way of bringing out the best in everybody.

The same day Vishy was batting for the State Bank in August 1988, national newspapers were carrying the latest syndicated column by his brother-in-law and fellow batting genius, Sunil Gavaskar. This column talked of two benefit matches in which Gavaskar had lately participated, in Lancashire and Toronto respectively, and reflected *en passant* on a BBC interview where the great man had been asked to explain England's dismal showing against West Indian pace. Of course, Gavaskar has been loyal to his club, Dadar Union, and city-state, Bombay, while Viswanath has had his share of international exposure. But for me the day's juxtapositions illustrated what the two had made of their respective careers. While Vishy returned to the ambience of his home town and bank job on the termination of his Test career, Gavaskar made what was for him an equally logical transition towards becoming the elder statesman of world cricket. Whereas one had used his cricketing prowess to achieve a status normally reserved for film stars, the other had enjoyed his playing days to the full and returned quietly to the surroundings from whence he came. Both paths are entirely legitimate, yet the contrast is instructive.

It is indeed remarkable how often in the history of Test cricket have such pairs of batsmen emerged to play for their country. Think for example of the Australian contemporaries Don Bradman and Stan McCabe. Bradman, like Gavaskar, was cool, collected, and kept his own counsel; an avid record breaker and astute captain on the field, a single-minded, but totally ethical, businessman off it. McCabe, like Vishy, was blessed with a sunny temperament and made friends easily, and played his strokes with little concern for the record books. (Yet it fell to him to play three of the greatest innings in the history of Test cricket.) In fact, when McCabe was asked why he didn't write his autobiography, he replied—'because I do not hate anybody enough'—a remark that could just as easily have been made by Viswanath. Or think again of the taciturn Len Hutton and the exuberant Denis Compton, who between them held together England's batting for twenty years. J.M. Kilburn, himself a Yorkshireman and an admirer of Hutton, once wrote: 'Hutton's name is austerely untouched by anecdote. He is the greatest living batsman and—behind this—he is the greatest living batsman. . . . Hutton has never given the public any cosy human view of himself which will allow them to recognize him as *mon semblable, mon frere* (a brother and fellow human being), capable, however rarely, of the same errors of nerve and judgement as themselves'. Compare this with what

Robertson-Glasgow had to say of Compton: 'No athlete of modern times has been so popular with the young. The shout that greets Denis Compton when he walks out to bat is mainly of treble and alto pitch. He is, of course what each shouter would himself like to be. . . .' *

Kilburn and Robertson-Glasgow could have been writing about the personalities of the great Indian dúo, with two caveats—while Hutton was grim to the last, Gavaskar has unwound after retirement to emerge as a most pleasing media personality; and unlike the experience of Compton, not only the young but also the middle-aged and elderly identified whole-heartedly with Viswanath.

What, then, of their respective cricketing gifts? In a Test at Bangalore against Asif Iqbal's Pakistanis, I watched a rare partnership between the two. Sitting behind me were three gentlemen in their fifties, all resplendent in navy-blue blazers bearing the insignia of the Andhra Pradesh Cricket Association. Gavaskar's exquisite forward play and controlled driving didn't seem to appeal to them, but they went into raptures whenever Vishy square cut Abdul Qadir, which was often. Each time he sent the ball to the left, or right, of point, the three gentlemen would break out into a smile as broad as the mouth of the river Krishna, roll their heads from side to side, and sing in unison: 'Aaaah, Vishwaaaa!'

But were these Andhra gentlemen right? In this connection, the Gavaskar-Viswanath comparison has always reminded me of the not dissimilar comparison between the sitar wizards Ravi Shankar and Vilayat Khan. While the vast majority of cricket lovers, who couldn't tell a square cut from a square drive, prefer Gavaskar, the vast majority of music lovers, who with difficulty would distinguish the sitar from the sarod,

* See Scyld Berry, *The Observer Book of Cricket* (Unwin, 1988), pp 11-14.

94

obviously prefer Ravi Shankar. This then is the 'received wisdom', which is not received very kindly by those who follow cricket or music more seriously. The cricket connoisseur believes Vishy, on account of the greater variety of his shots, to be the better player, just as the person who has studied music plumps unreservedly for Vilayat, a man capable of inspired bursts of genius. Of course, the choice of these self-styled connoisseurs is dictated to a large extent by the desire to distance themselves from the crowd. Actually, the practitioners in both professions echo the majority sentiment—just ask any bowler who he'd prefer to bowl to, or any musician who s/he would prefer to play after. (Not that anyone would welcome the choice, for Vilayat knows a thing or two about the sitar, and Vishy couldn't half bat!)

But there is something to be said for the minority choice. Where Ravi Shankar and Gavaskar play confidently on the world's stage, Vilayat and Vishy have dug deep roots in their home turf. The loyalty of the Calcutta music fans to Vilayat is matched only by the esteem in which Vishy is held among cricket lovers in Bangalore. Like his compatriot B.S. Chandrasekhar, but for somewhat different reasons, Viswanath is a man universally loved and admired, certainly by his peers but above all by his home crowd.

One reason for this attachment is the man's character; another is his services to Karnataka cricket. I write a little later of the hundred he scored in the historic victory over Bombay in 1974. Another hundred of scarcely less significance was made against Delhi in the Ranji Trophy semi-final five years later. In Karnataka's reply to Delhi's first innings score of 332, wickets fell steadily, mostly to Bishen Bedi, while Vishy stroked fluently at the other end. While he was frequently troubled by quickish left-arm spinners such as Underwood and Iqbal Qasim, Vishy was more at home against the flighted stuff, and had in

95

particular an impressive record against Bedi and Delhi. This time, the Sardar quickly realized that Vishy would get Karnataka the crucial first-innings lead before he got the others out, and the only hope, albeit a slender one, lay in the new ball. (At the time, Delhi boasted India's new ball pair, Madan Lal and Mohinder Amarnath.) Mohinder's first delivery with the red cherry was a shortish outswinger, which Vishy cut past point for four. Mohinder then tried an inswinger, pitching it up to give the ball more time to swing, and Vishy pivoted on his left foot, opened his chest and drove it past mid-on. 'Hazare!' exulted the man in the seat next to mine (the former Ranji Trophy player and well known cricket writer Sujit Mukherjee), 'only Hazare could play the on drive like that'. These sentiments seem to have been echoed by Bedi, ruefully chewing a blade of grass at mid-on. His bolt had been shot, and he knew it—those two strokes were the last nails in Delhi's coffin.

My mind went back to those two boundaries as I watched Vishy bat in what turned out to be his last first-class innings on his home ground, against Tamil Nadu in March 1988. I could barely hold back the tears (nor probably, could Viswanath) as, for one last time, the crackers exploded in the west stand of the Chinnaswamy Stadium, as his fans welcomed him—in the way they had done down the years—in symbolic anticipation of his blazing strokeplay. Vishy played defensively forward to his first ball, and was caught at short left off the third—but in between he had unleashed his famous square-cut, appropriately enough his last scoring stroke for Karnataka in Karnataka.

IV

Prasanna made his debut for Mysore in 1960, Chandrasekhar three years later. Yet it took another decade for Mysore to come anywhere near winning the Ranji Trophy. For Mysore to have

96

any realistic hope of beating Bombay, they needed at least two batsmen who could score big hundreds consistently and against any attack. The first of these, Viswanath himself, came along late in the decade. Some discerning cricket lovers know that every one of Vishy's fourteen Test hundreds either saved India from defeat or else put it on the road to victory; not one was made in a match India lost. Even fewer people realize that Vishy's career coincided with his state's ascendancy in Indian cricket; for, while he played, no fewer than three Ranji championships came to adorn what was previously a bare cupboard.

The historic occasion when all these talents came together was the Ranji Trophy semi-final against Bombay in March 1974. Karnataka began in most inauspicious fashion. Off the second ball of the match, Abdul Ismail had the dangerous Vijaykumar caught at slip. In came Vishy, to a thundering reception. (Those were the days when upto 30,000 watched important Ranji Trophy matches.) He was hopelessly beaten by the first ball, a sharp inswinger that thudded low into his pads. It would I swear have uprooted all three stumps, but to the disbelief of the Bombay side, and perhaps on the theory that Test cricketers must always be given the benefit of doubt on their first ball, the umpire gave Viswanath not out—and even Vishy wasn't going to walk on a leg-before call. The maestro did not make another mistake, crafting a majestic 162 studded with the most delicate late cuts off Shivalkar and the off-spinner Milind Rege.

As the Bombay attack wilted, along came the second batsman Karnataka had been waiting for all these years— Brijesh Parasuram Patel. Patel came from a well-known cricketing family; at least four of his uncles and one cousin played for Mysore. (His father, Parasuram Patel, was a promising cricketer who had his career cut short by a major accident—a cripple thereafter, he was until his recent death a familiar sight, in his wheelchair, at matches in Bangalore.) As for Brijesh himself, he scored at a rate of knots against all but the very best attacks—his only perceptible weakness was against genuine pace, and in a helmeted age he would have overcome even that deficiency. For Karnataka his bludgeoning strokeplay made an effective contrast to Vishy's artistry, and on this occasion his rapid 112 saw his team safely past the 400 mark.

But was 400 enough? Prasanna wasn't sure, and while he kept one end going when Bombay batted, he alternated Chandrasekhar with N. Laxman, a defensive left-hander in the Nadkarni mould, playing his first Ranji season at the age of forty. The first hurdle was the great Gavaskar. Pras fed him on his favourite on drive, and then bowled a ball of full length which, just as the batsman was making to drive, swerved abruptly in its flight to take the off bail. I can still see Gavaskar clapping his hand against his bat as he left the ground, in acknowledgement of Prasanna's wizardry.

But Gavaskar's exit brought in a man even more feared in the Ranji Trophy, Ajit Wadekar. The Karnataka captain now decided to play a waiting game, and immediately posted a deep point and deep third man, in recognition of the most savage square cut in Indian cricket. When they batted together for upwards of three hours, it looked as if there was nothing to stop Wadekar and his partner, Ashok Mankad, but time and fortune were on the side of the Karnataka skipper. 'Kaka' Mankad played a ball into the off side, Wadekar advanced for a single, only to be sent back by his partner as Sudhakar Rao advanced quickly from point. Ajit turned, slipped, and just failed to make his ground. And Prasanna, who had been waiting for this moment the better part of a lifetime, was over the bails to take Sudhakar's throw.

Wadekar's dismissal was the turning point, for even Pras

knew that the most likely way the Bombay captain would get out, with history and honour at stake, was through a fluke such as this. (Wadekar, like Gavaskar, Solkar and Bombay batsmen more generally, was a masterly judge of the short single, and if he hadn't slipped he would still be batting at the Chinnaswamy stadium.) As Wadekar walked grimly off the ground, he little realized that this was only the beginning of the bad luck that was to plague him all year. culminating in the ignominy of India's three-nil defeat under his leadership in England that summer.

However, Prasanna and Karnataka had still to contend with Mankad, Eknath Solkar, Milind Rege, etc., but they chipped steadily away. A minor flutter was raised by a ninth wicket stand between the splendidly named Bandiwadekar, the Bombay stumper, and a still outraged Abdul Ismail, which took the score past 300. (At this stage, convinced that Bombay would come through, my uncle put his head in his hands and groaned, 'the blighters have escaped again'.) But Pras wasn't going to let this one get away, and he returned to polish off the innings, ending with a match-winning 5 for 117 off a marathon 62 overs.

Bombay's innings ended early on the last day. As Karnataka played out time, news came of a piece of luck as astonishing, and welcome, as Wadekar's run out, relayed to us by the Indian cricket lover's most constant friend, All India Radio. In the other semi-final, Jaisimha's Hyderabad had been put out by Rajasthan, a victory as improbable as the Rajputs defeating the massed might of the Mughals. The unlikely hero of this triumph was an Air Force officer on loan to his native Rajasthan, G.S. Shaktawat. An off-spinner with a jerky action bordering on the illegitimate, Shaktawat took 6 for 24 as Hyderabad made a mess of a small victory target. Prasanna was beside himself with delight, for he knew Abid Ali, Pataudi, Jaisimha and company to be an infinitely more difficult proposition than the knights of Rajasthan—and so it turned out, with Karnataka running out easy winners in the final at Jaipur.

To gauge precisely what Karnataka's win over Bombay meant, we may quickly go over earlier Ranji Trophy semi-finals between the two teams. In March 1964 they played at Bangalore, and after Karnataka, then playing as Mysore, had been bowled out for 155, Prasanna and Chandrasekhar had Bombay at 78 for 4, before Ajit Wadekar with an innings of 127 took his side to a commanding lead and eventual victory. Three years later they played at Bombay, when, in a match I have mentioned in a previous chapter, Wadekar, with a triple hundred, nearly equalled the Mysore score off his own bat. In 1970 they met a third time, and after Mysore had scored as many as 309, Bombay replied with 520 for 8—centuries by Dilip Sardesai and Eknath Solkar, with Wadekar contributing a mere 91 (Pras's bowling figures were 25/7/74/0, Chandra's 50/4/181/2.) Finally, two years before the match I have just described, Bombay batted first and scored 257, which on a turning track was adequate for a comfortable victory, the left-arm spinner, Shivalkar, wrecking the Mysore batting with match figures of 13 wickets for 50 runs.

The 1974 semi-final, therefore, was the fifth such encounter in ten years, with Bombay winning the first four without so much as a hiccup. With due respect to Vishy, Brijesh, Chandra and Pras, clearly supernatural forces were responsible for this unexpected turn-up of the form book—notably Wadekar's footwear, and the right index finger of the umpire, which remained stuck inside his pocket when Ismail appeared to have Vishy l.b.w. first ball. The last word shall be with this gentleman from Calcutta, who went back home and boasted to the Bengal cricketers: 'I have done what you people could not do all these years—made sure that Bombay does not win the Ranji Trophy'.

100

*1. Engineer's (and Kunderan's) worthy successor 2 & 3. Two
millionares of spin 4. The other Little Master*

V

Through all this, the fourth member of Karnataka's brilliant quartet was carrying on his duties behind and before the stumps in his customarily self-effacing manner. That discerning judge, Tiger Pataudi, has recently noted that Syed Kirmani was the best Indian stumper of his experience, and I see no reason to quarrel with that verdict. But in his long apprenticeship as Engineer's understudy, 'Kiri' must have wondered whether the flamboyant Parsi would ever retire, though as it turned out he came to enjoy a long tenure (1975–85, with the odd interruption) as India's number one stumper. One piece of good fortune was the emergence of Kapil Dev, so Kiri could show the world that Indian keepers could handle fast bowlers too. I was privileged to see the two brilliant leg-side catches he took the first day of the Madras Test in 1980, sending the Pakistani openers Mudassar and Sadiq on their way and preparing the ground for a famous win. Three years later, he took two brilliant off-side catches off seaming deliveries to dismiss Gower and Bacchus at crucial stages of the semi-final and final of the 1983 World Cup.

Despite his familiarity with swing and cut, the hallmark of Kirmani's keeping, in the Indian tradition, was his expert handling of spin bowling—only to be expected of one weaned on Prasanna and Chandrasekhar. In the first Test against Pakistan in 1979–80, Zaheer Abbas, the scourge of India's spin in the previous series between the two sides, was batting beautifully when Doshi came on to bowl. In the left-armer's first over Zaheer swept and drove him for boundaries—going for another sweep off the last ball, he fractionally overbalanced and Kiri had the bails off. This particular stumping was among the most important Kiri ever made, for if Zaheer had carried on he would most likely have dominated the match and series.

As it happened, that dismissal signalled a loss of form so abrupt that Zaheer was dropped from the Pakistan side before the series was over.

At forty, Kirmani is still superbly fit and playing for the Railways. He shifted sides because Karnataka chose to promote the talented youngster S. Viswanath, but for a while Kiri carried on as a batsman. In his last season with his home side, I watched him make top score on a brute of a wicket against the old enemy, Tamil Nadu. Later, as Tamil Nadu struggled against the eventual match-winner Raghuram Bhatt, more than one spectator wished that Kiri, with his always outsize pads, was where he wished most to be. As S. Viswanath missed a difficult leg-side stumping off Bhatt and let the ball go for four byes besides, a section of the west stand gave vent to their feelings. The cry of 'we want Kirmani' went up, an understandable request but a bit hard on the young Viswanath, trying hard for a comeback to the national side.*

VI

I wonder if the Bangalore crowd ever turned on Kirmani in his early days. For he succeeded another popular and entertaining cricketer as Mysore's wicket-keeper–batsman, Budhi Kunderan. Budhi, who now lives in Scotland, went to school in Bombay where he was taken in hand by the well-known Parsi coach Homi Vajifdar. He made his first-class debut for the Railways, whose captain Lala Amarnath, recommended him for the Indian side. Making his Test debut against Australia in 1959, over the next decade he alternated as India's keeper with Farokh Engineer, in a lively but wholly amicable rivalry. De-

---

*As this book goes to press, there is news of Kirmani's return to the Karnataka Ranji Trophy Team, as batsman, wicket-keeper—and captain.

spite his early cricketing affiliations, Kunderan was born at Mulki on Karnataka's west coast and played several seasons for the state, so we are well within our rights to consider him here. As likely as Srikkanth to hit the first ball of a Test match for four or six, Budhi once scored over 500 runs in a series against England. Indeed, he would walk into an all-time state side on the strength of his batting alone. As befitting a champion schoolboy athlete, Kunderan was a fine outfielder, and here we could even persuade him to bowl the ritual overs with the new ball in preparation for Prasanna and Chandrasekhar, a task that fell to him when both Engineer and he were picked for the Edgbaston Test in 1967.

Although the ebullient Vijaykumar would run him close, as Budhi's opening partner for a mythical Mysore XI one must choose the late Benjamin Frank, a legendary hitter equally at home opening the innings or in the middle order. As an all-round fielder, Frank was reckoned by his contemporaries to be every bit as good as Gul Mahommed or Hemu Adhikari. A part-time wicket-keeper too, in his youth he had also been a crack inside-right at hockey, in which game his shot at goal had all the explosive power of his on drive in cricket. Above all, Frank is remembered in Bangalore as a man of enormous charm, with a West Indian temperament both on and off the field. No wonder that Frank was gifted a gold watch by the great Everton Weekes when he played a brilliant innings of 123 for East Zone at Allahabad against John Goddard's side of 1948-9. Frank's innings, along with Shute Bannerjee's eleven wickets in the match, was instrumental in the West Indies suffering their only defeat of the tour. Frank's hitting in that match was not easily forgotten by the Allahabad crowd. Several years later, when Frank's colleague P.S. Viswanath took a University team to play in the holy city, they were told in loving detail of their townsman's innings against the West Indies.

Frank had in fact a quite outstanding record against touring teams. For East Zone against the M.C.C. tourists of 1951–2, Frank top-scored in both innings (98 not out of a total of 158, 75 out of 228). The next winter, he hit a blazing 93 at a run a minute against the visiting Pakistanis, an innings studded with no less than fourteen fours and three sixes. Men have been capped for India for much lesser deeds, but inexplicably Frank never played a Test.

The only time Frank failed against a touring side was when he came up against the expatriate Australian George Tribe. Tribe, the greatest ever left-arm wrist-spinner (yes, better even than Gary Sobers), toured India with two Commonwealth teams in the early fifties, and his mastery of Rusi Modi effectively ended the Parsi stylist's international career. Like Modi and a few others, Frank couldn't tell Tribe's chinaman from his googly. Playing for the Bengal Governor's XI against the Commonwealth side, Frank shouldered arms to what he thought was a googly—only it was a chinaman and wrecked his stumps. Frank loved telling this story against himself, so much so that to this day cases of batsmen being bowled shouldering arms in the Bangalore leagues are known simply as 'Frank judgements'.

These varied escapades against touring sides all happened when Frank played for a few years as a professional for Calcutta's Mohun Bagan Club, and hence for Bengal and East Zone. However, after playing as a boy of nineteen in the Bombay Pentangular, Frank made his debut for Mysore in the next year, 1940. He was bowled for a duck by the left-arm spinner A.G. Ram Singh, but in later years played some punishing innings for Mysore against Madras. A friend remembers watching a Mysore–Madras match in the early forties when Frank repeatedly late cut Ram Singh past an astonished C.P. Johnstone at slip—for, like another great hitter, Kapil Dev,

Frank could cut delicately too. On returning from Bengal, he resumed his place at the top of the Mysore batting, and played league cricket well into the nineteen-sixties. (His son, Sydney, was a firm-footed hitter like the father, who would surely have played for the state but for a serious leg injury.) A most genial man who had a special place for young cricketers, Frank was as much an adornment to Mysore cricket as Chandra and Vishy.

VII

Our mythical Mysore opening pair of Kunderan and Frank would be an apt answer to Tamil Nadu's Srikkanth and Ramaswami (see Chapter Six), a partnership guaranteed to empty out even Bangalore's most popular eating house, the fabled Mavalli Tiffin Rooms or MTR. One of the remaining batting places in an all-time Mysore XI would be capably filled by V. Subrahmanyam. For the other, one cannot dismiss lightly the claims of P.A. Kanickam, known as the South Indian Hobbs in the days before the Ranji Trophy. Mushtaq Ali, who played against Kanickam in the latter's declining years, wrote with feeling of his off-side wizardry. Nor have I forgotten the considerable batting talents of L.T. Adisesh and P.S. Viswanath from the nineteen fifties and P.R. Ashokanand and Salus Nazareth from the nineteen-sixties. However, I shall yield to the temptation of smuggling in another member of the Ranji Trophy winning side of 1974. But Sudhakar Rao has earned his place. A marvellous player of spin bowling, he got scant opportunities on his only tour as an India player, of New Zealand and the West Indies in 1975–6. As for the all-rounder's spot, it would be graced by the first Anglo Indian to play cricket for the country, Roger Binny. A first-rate team man, Binny played a leading part in two victorious invasions of England, the World Cup campaign of 1983 and the Test series three years later.

We still have room for one bowler. Seam bowling candidates include Brijesh's cousin Y.B. Patel, left-arm inswing, and G. Kasturirangan, right-arm inswing, bowled off the wrong foot. Kasturirangan, who turned down an invitation to tour the West Indies with the Indian side in the early fifties, may be best remembered for his contribution, in his professional capacity as a horticulturist, towards preparing the wicket and outfield at the Chinnaswamy Stadium. But perhaps we need a third spinner to take the load off Prasanna and Chandrasekhar, especially if Mysore were to play Bombay in our mythical competition. Think for example of B.K. Garudachar, the leg-spinner who held most of Mysore's bowling records till Chandra came along, and who must surely have played for India if his Brahmin family hadn't insisted that an engineering degree was more important than cricket. (With Frank and the stylish C.J. Ramdev, Garudachar led Mysore into the final of the Ranji Trophy in 1941–2 when they lost, predictably, to Bombay.) Or think, again, of P.E. Palia, the Parsi left-armer who played in India's first Test, and moved to Mysore after many years with U.P. A wristy strokeplayer with the bat, as a bowler Palia, *à la* Wilfred Rhodes, preferred to begin with the new ball. And for sheer length of service, one cannot easily overlook Raghuram Bhatt, still the most prodigious spinner of the ball in the country, and distinctly unlucky to be capped only twice for India. Above all these worthy cricketers, my own fancy is for another man who, like Bhatt, played only twice for India—V.M. Muddiah. A skilful off-spinner and fine student of the game, Muddiah's infrequent Test appearance were solely a consequence of his overlapping with Ghulam Ahmed and Jasu Patel. Starting out with Mysore, he then played many years, as an Air

Force officer, for the Services. Among his considerable feats, he treasures most the match in which he dismissed the great Lala Amarnath for two low scores.

As the first home-bred spinner from Mysore to play for India, Muddiah was, appropriately, one of the radio commentators when Karnataka beat Bombay for the first time. During one of his breaks off the air, we ran into him in the pavilion. My uncle introduced me as a schoolboy off-spinner who wished to take tips from him. Muddiah pointed to the match in progress and to the bowler, Prasanna, saying 'son, there's the master off spinner—you will learn more watching him today than I could teach you in a dozen coaching sessions.' Who said cricketers are not generous?

VIII

Picking an all-time Karnataka XI has been almost as difficult as picking one for Bombay, even though I haven't considered at all the rich stream of Mysore exiles who played for Madras—such as B.S. Alva, A.S. Krishnaswamy, K.R. Rajagopal, Najam Hussain, P.K. Beliappa and P. Mukund. (This migration, by the way, reserves the historic Madras–Mysore migration of all the four varnas—priests, soldiers, merchants and labourers.) But my friends in Bangalore, though equally absorbed with the game, are more forgiving. They will even allow me to change my mind yet again, and substitute Sudhakar Rao by the more versatile Palia. So my all-time Karnataka XI reads

1. B.K. Kunderan
2. B. Frank
3. G.R. Viswanath
4. V. Subrahmanyam (captain)
5. B.P. Patel

6. P.E. Palia
7. R.M.H. Binny
8. S.M.H. Kirmani (wicket-keeper)
9. V.M. Muddiah
10. E.A.S. Prasanna
11. B.S. Chandrasekhar
12th man: Sudhakar Rao

Alternatively, one could opt *in toto* for the side that dethroned Bombay in 1974 which in batting order read: 1. V.S. Vijaykumar 2. Sanjay Desai 3. G.R. Viswanath 4. B.P. Patel 5. Sudhakar Rao 6. A.V. Jayaprakash 7. S.M.H. Kirmani 8. B. Vijaykrishna 9. E.A.S. Prasanna (captain) 10. N. Laxman 11. B.S. Chandrasekhar 12th man and reserve wicket-keeper: B. Raghunath

No portrait of Karnataka cricket would be complete without a mention of its Grand Old Man, M. Chinnaswamy. Now a sprightly eighty-five, in his seventies Chinnaswamy supervised, brick by brick, the construction of the stadium that now bears his name. Chinnaswamy is an institution of which Mysore cricket is justly proud. So are M.G. Vijaysarathy and M.V. Nagendra, the only father-and-son pair to have umpired in Test cricket. Vijaysarathy's own father, M.A. Sreenivasa Rao, was in his own time a cricketing institution in Bangalore. A much loved Professor of Chemistry at the city's Central College, he was prone to giving advice during matches to the college cricket team, from under a tree at square leg.

CHAPTER SIX

Tamils and Turbans
in Triplicane

*T*he social life of the Madras locality of Triplicane
revolves around two venerable institutions: the
Parthasarathy temple and the Chepauk Cricket
Ground. Some years ago, the Parthasarathy
temple was rocked by an unseemly controversy between the
two subcastes of Iyengar Brahmins who form its main clientele.
Whereas the Vadagalai Iyengars, who endowed the shrine,
insisted the temple elephant wear their caste mark on the
forehead during the great Dasera procession, the Thengalai
Iyengars claimed that, as the temple priest came from its ranks,
the beast must wear the Thengalai stamp. The case dragged
relentlessly on (reported in detail by that other great Iyengar
institution, *The Hindu*), with the Vadagalais winning the first
round in the District Court and the Thengalais successfully
appealing in the High Court. While the Supreme Court in New
Delhi deliberated on its verdict—against which there could be
no appeal—the elephant decided to have the final say, and
dropped dead.

Iyengar Brahmins are reckoned by anthropologists to be
the most exclusive of communities in a social hierarchy generally obsessed with purity and pollution. However, when not
agitating over elephant caste marks the two subcastes of Iyengars

live in comparative amity—especially on the cricket field. A writer who has followed Madras cricket for half a century, T.G. Vaidyanathan, first drew my attention to the 'distinctly Iyengar complexion of Chepauk crowds'. In fact, not only have the Vadagalais and Thengalais closed ranks in this sphere, but the Iyengars as a whole have forged a historic compromise with the rival Brahmin caste of Iyers. Between them, Iyengars and Iyers dominate the cricketing landscape of Tamil Nadu. The state's cricketing administrators are overwhelmingly Brahmin, as are its most involved spectators, while in an average Ranji Trophy side Brahmin representation is well out of proportion to their share in the general population.

II

Madras's first great cricketer was inevitably an Iyengar, M.J. Gopalan. Gopalan, who came from a poor Brahmin household, took employment initially in the Madras Police before the Englishman, C.P. Johnstone, gave him a job in his own company, Burmah Shell. (A stodgy left-hand batsman, the Cambridge Blue Johnstone was Madras's first captain in the Ranji Trophy.) His sporting genius, however, needed no recommendation, and in 1936 Gopalan was faced with the unenviable choice of accompanying the Indian hockey team to the Berlin Olympics or going with the Indian cricket team on their English tour. Gopalan, perhaps unwisely, chose the latter. For if he had gone to Berlin he would have returned with a gold medal, whereas in England the seam bowling trio of Nissar, Amar Singh and Jahangir Khan put paid to his chances of Test selection.

The only Test Gopalan played in was against Jardine's touring side of 1933–4. When he played hockey for India against New Zealand the following winter, Gopalan narrowly beat his close friend and fellow townsman C. Ramaswami to the honour of being the country's first double international. Gopalan entered big cricket as a fast bowler, carrying his Iyengar caste marks of the *naamam* (white paste, trident shaped, on forehead) and *kudumi* (pigtail) on to the cricket field. The *naamam* was no hindrance, but as the *kudumi* would get loose while bowling, Gopalan invariably played with a close-fitting black cap. The cosmopolitan C. Ramaswami—who had crossed the polluting Kala Pani to go to Cambridge and was a non-Brahmin to boot—persuaded M.J. to dispense with the *kudumi* altogether. Gopalan initially resisted, relenting only when he was safely out of Madras with Ramaswami on a cricket tour of Bombay. By the time he bowled the first ball of the first match in the Ranji Trophy, the *kudumi* was a tail of the past.

In time, Gopalan developed into a free-driving hitter in the C.K. Nayudu mould (no doubt Ramaswami had a hand in this as well). When he came in to bat at Chepauk, the crowd sang him all the way to the wicket, chanting 'Gopalaa, Gopalaa', a traditional incantation in honour of that favourite Iyengar deity, Lord Krishna. He rarely disappointed his admirers. One of his last flourishes was a hard-hitting half century as captain of South Zone against the West Indies in 1949.

Gopalan's closest disciple was another Iyengar fast bowler, C.R. Rangachari. Like his mentor, Rangachari also played his early years attached to his *kudumi* and worked in the Madras Police. (It is easy to imagine policemen as fast bowlers—others of the ilk include the Ceylon tearaway of the nineteen-sixties, Kehelgamuwa, and Ghulam Guard of Bombay. Of course Gary Sobers bowled both fast and slow, but then he worked not on the beat but as a musician in the police band.) On the Australian tour of 1947, Rangachari had Bradman badly missed by Amarnath at slip before the Don had scored. However, the Brahmin who nearly bowled Bradman did the next best thing by bowling the Black Bradman the following winter. In the Delhi Test of that year, 'Ranga' had the West Indies reeling at 27 for 3, claiming the wickets of Jeffrey Stollmeyer, Alan Rae and George Headley—as good a trio as any—at a personal cost of one run. Centuries by Gomez, Christiani, Walcott, and Weekes (Worrell was not on that tour) took the West Indies to 631, but Rangachari's figures were a heroic 5 for 107 off 30 overs. The ball with which he bowled Headley splintered the master's off-stump. This great triumph has passed into Madras folklore, and in fact the broken stump was displayed for years afterwards in the Ferozeshah Kotla pavilion.

III

Iyengar Brahmins have continued to hold sway over Madras cricket. A colourful Iyengar contemporary of Gopalan and Rangachari was the googly bowler turned journalist turned diplomat, G. Parathasarthi. Notable Iyengar cricketers since the Second World War include the Mysore exiles K.R. Rajagopal (a wicket-keeper-batsman) and P. Mukund (an inswing bowler like his uncle, G. Kasturirangan); the leg-spinner in the Ranji Trophy winning side of 1955, A.K. Sarangapani; and the Test batsmen T.E. Srinivasan and W.V. Raman. However, the two great Iyengar cricketers of modern times are also the only Tamilians to have captained India, S. Venkataraghavan and K. Srikkanth.

Venkataraghavan was unexpectedly thrust into the national captaincy in the last weeks of 1974, when India had lost four Tests in a row. After the captain, Pataudi, and the vice-captain, Gavaskar, had reported unfit for the Delhi Test against the West Indies, the president of the local association, Ram Prakash Mehra, announced at a reception on the eve of the match that Farokh Engineer was to lead the home side. This announcement, widely reported in the newspapers, clearly did not have the backing of the Cricket Board, for next morning the crowd was astonished to see 'Venkat' coming out to toss with Clive Lloyd. The signs were unpropitious, and it had to be a decision against Venkat that cost India the match. After scoring a modest 220, the home team recovered to have the West Indies at 120 for 4, but Vivian Richards was given not out when palpably caught behind off the India captain. Richards went on to score 192 not out, and India lost by an innings.

When Chandrasekhar was reinstated for the next Text, Venkat reverted to twelfth man. Captain one match, twelfth man the next: surely a unique transition in the history of Test cricket. But then Venkat was always a remarkably unselfish cricketer. Of the great spin quartet, he was unfortunately the least glamorous (only cricketing-wise, that is, for he was by far the best looking of the four) lacking Bedi's consummate flight, Prasanna's variations, and Chandrasekhar's turn and bounce. But in at least three respects he outdid his more famous comrades. While Chandra was no more than adequate in the field, and Bedi and Prasanna (to borrow a phrase) were both stately on the run, Venkat was one of the finest fielders who ever played for India. In the leg trap he was almost as good as Solkar, while at slip—as the crucial catch to dismiss Brian Luckhurst in the 1971 Oval Test showed—he was unequalled. Again, alone among the quartet, Venkat was comfortable bowling to left-handers. The great Clive Lloyd always played him with uncharacteristic caution, while Venkat delayed Alvin Kallicharan's entry into Test cricket by at least a year. Finally, and this is an accurate reflection on the man's services to the game, the Tamil off-spinner was the most long-serving of the four.

When one thinks of the staying power of Wilfred Rhodes or Vinoo Mankad, it is indeed surprising that Bedi's international career lasted barely twelve years, Chandrasekhar's fifteen, and Prasanna's sixteen (and mind you, all made their Test debut at a very young age). Eighteen years after his own Test debut, Venkat was a strong contender for the 1982 England tour. It was rumoured that Gavaskar, who had succeeded Venkat as captain, did not want him, so the wily Cho Ramaswamy, the editor of the well known Tamil magazine *Tughlak*, appealed to Gavaskar in the pages of a widely circulated English weekly. There had been much loose talk, wrote Cho, of a provincial rivalry between Bombay and Madras and an individual rivalry between Gavaskar and Venkat. Such gossip was insulting to Gavaskar's intellect, said the writer, for even if Sunil and Venkat were not the best of friends the former knew that it would ultimately resound to the team's and his benefit if the off-spinner was there to lead the attack. This shrewd appeal to instrumental reason did not work, for Venkat did not go on what would have been his fifth tour of England. He was then surprisingly selected, despite Cho's silence, for the tour of the West Indies the next year. In this, his farewell bow in international cricket, Venkat was the toast of the Caribbean commentators, who spoke feelingly of the 'wily Venkat, full of guile', and the 'amazin' reflexes at slip of a thirty-eight-year-old man'.

Venkat was an intellectual among cricketers, and, as an 'informed' source once informed me, he alone among an Indian touring side to Pakistan wanted to visit Harappa and Mohenjodaro. His scholarly demeanour won him a reputation among his fellow players for arrogance, but on occasion he could be very generous indeed. After the thrashing in Pakistan in 1978 had effectively ended the careers of Bedi, Chandrasekhar and Prasanna, Venkat seemed set for a long spell as India's main spin bowler. The new captain, Gavaskar, followed those tough Yorkshiremen Len Hutton and Ray

Illingworth in the belief that only seam bowling won Test
matches, and the economical Venkat played to perfection the
role of the one spinner this scheme allowed in the series that
followed the Pakistan debacle, against a West Indian side badly
depleted by the exertions of Kerry Packer. I watched the Delhi
Test, when the West Indies were bowled out for under 200 after
India had run up a score of 550 for 6 declared. Karsan Ghavri
and Kapil Dev had run through the top order, while Venkat
and Chandrasekhar (recalled for this match) mopped up the
tail. Unsurprisingly, the fast bowlers were asked to lead the
team in, and as Ghavri and Kapil, like a pair of prize fighters—
Ghavri indeed looked and acted like one—walked victoriously
off the field, I said to myself: 'That's the end of the Golden Age
of Spin'. Venkat was following on the heels of the feisty duo, but
he suddenly stopped at the pavilion gate and turned round to
see the shy, nervous Chandrasekhar bringing up the rear with
his Karnataka teammate, the wicket-keeper Syed Kirmani.
Where the rest of the team and the crowd itself had eyes only
for Ghavri and Kapil, Venkat caught Chandra's eye and clapped
his hands in applause. Indian cricket may no longer have had
much place for the art of spin, but Venkat would not abandon
his fellow craftsmen.

Like Venkat, the other Iyengar to captain India was not
allowed an extended reign as captain, being surprisingly sacked
after drawing a Test series in Pakistan which the pundits had
confidently predicted India would lose four-nil. However,
crowds in at least seven countries will remember
Krishnamachari Srikkanth with affection as the most thrilling
of modern batsmen. It has been well said of the Madras opener
that he is the only Tamil Brahmin for whom security is not a
watchword. Srikkanth's first major score in Test cricket was a
half century at Bangalore against Keith Fletcher's Englishmen
in 1981–2. In that innings, his audacious strokeplay was inter-

rupted only by repeated mid-wicket conferences with his partner and skipper, Sunil Gavaskar, who at the end of every over
asked Srikkanth to be more discerning in the choice of balls to
hit. The youngster would nod vigorously in assent (left to right,
in the Tamil style) only to immediately slog Botham over the
infield. Gavaskar soon gave up in exasperation. In later years,
far from admonishing his partner, Gavaskar would smile indul-
gently at the other end as Srikkanth flouted every rule in the
book and more often as not got away with it.

Early on in his career, Srikkanth challenged one of the
conventional pieties of one-day cricket—namely that not losing a wicket, rather than scoring runs, was the name of the
game in its early overs. He was prone to send the first delivery
of a match whistling over the bowler's head. Undoubtedly, his
lofted drives in the starting overs of an innings—off Joel
Garner and Bob Willis, Richard Hadlee and Imran Khan—
rank as one of the most radical innovations of the limited-overs
game. Srikkanth is also one of the very few cricketers to have
had an influence on Gavaskar, the man apparently born with
a perfect technique and dazzling array of strokes. In his first
one-day international, Gavaskar scored 36 not out in sixty
overs; in one of his last, against New Zealand at Nagpur in 1987,
he hit one of the fastest centuries in the history of one-day
cricket. As Gavaskar acknowledged, it was the experience of
batting opposite Srikkanth that made this transformation
possible.

Srikkanth's hitting in a minor match at Rawalpindi once
made Majid Khan's father, the normally reticent Jahangir
Khan, compare the Tamil to C.K. Nayudu and other great
hitters of his generation. However, unlike C.K., and Kapil Dev,
Srikkanth is far from being a classical hitter: his footwork is only
in the mind, his grip is too low, while the motive power is
provided by the right (i.e. wrong) hand. This idiosyncratic

A South Indian has at last become Prime Minister, but these two had already led India where it matters.

technique has not stopped him from playing some of the most exciting innings in modern cricket. The most valuable of the lot was perhaps his innings of 38 that turned out to be the highest individual score in the World Cup final of 1983. When he hooked Andy Roberts for four in the early overs of that match, the commentator Brian Johnstone said knowingly: 'That was Roberts' slow bouncer. Andy's just setting him up'. Roberts' fast bouncer duly arrived, and Srikkanth hooked it for six.

IV

The rivalry between Iyers and Iyengars in the fields of music, film and science has always been the subject of lively controversy. For example, the contributions of the mathematician and Iyengar, Srinivas Ramanujam, to the world of science are at least the equal of the physicist C.V. **Ram**an, an Iyer, while on the screen the charms of Meenakshi Seshadri (Iyer) are scarcely less than those of Hema Malini (Iyengar). And in the great tradition of Karnatik vocal music, Semangudi Srinivas Iyer is a worthy successor to Ariyakudi Ramanuja Iyengar.

But on the cricket field, at any rate, the Iyers must give way to the Iyengars. Indeed, the only Iyer cricketer of comparable class to the luminous Iyengar quartet was Venkat's old spinning mate, V.V. (Vaman) Kumar. An artist with the ball, like other great wrist-spinners (Gary Sobers and Abdul Qadir, for example) Kumar had two googlies, one for show, the other for real. He took five wickets in an innings on his Test debut against Pakistan, but after one failure against England the following winter he never played for India again— Chandrasekhar's arrival had something to do with this. But he led Tamil Nadu's attack for nearly two decades, and was the first bowler to take 400 wickets in the Ranji Trophy.

119

Kumar and Venkat were a duo just as difficult as Mysore's Prasanna and Chandrasekhar. They came to their peak in the early seventies, a time when Bombay's hold on the Ranji Trophy was visibly slipping, with their victory margins narrower by the year. Four teams, and four captains, were most threatening in their challenge—Karnataka under Prasanna, Hyderabad under Jaisimha, Rajasthan under Hanumant Singh, and Tamil Nadu under Venkat. When Tamil Nadu met Bombay in the Ranji Trophy final of 1972–3, Venkat instructed the Chepauk groundsman to prepare a turning track, confident that he, in combination with Kumar, would carry the day. Sure enough, Bombay, despite winning the toss, were dismissed for 160, and at the end of the first day Tamil Nadu were sitting pretty at 60 for 2. Next morning, Shivalkar and Solkar—in his original slow left-arm style—got to work, and the remaining eight wickets crumbled for next to nothing. Despite being dismissed for a comparatively low score the second time around (with ironically the *pace* bowler Kalyanasundaram getting a hat trick), Bombay won comfortably. As Venkat ruefully reflected: 'I knew Bombay would not get more than 150 on a turner against Kumar and myself, but I should have realized that on the same track Tamil Nadu were worth only half that amount'.

I do not know whether Kumar had any influence on his fellow Iyer, Laxman Sivaramakrishnan. As a leg-spinner, 'Siva' seemed to have it all—a classical sideways action, flight, turn and bounce. Sadly, unlike Kumar, the youngster seemed incapable of working long hours at the craft. As a seventeen-year-old, Siva took twelve wickets in winning a Test against England at Bombay, but he faded away thereafter. Despite some later successes in the pajama game, he remains a One-Test Wonder, reduced to playing for Tamil Nadu as a batsman and close in field.

An Iyer likely to be overlooked, owing to his self-effacing

120

manner, is the long-serving left-handed opener, V. Sivaramakrishnan. Sivaramakrishnan, who scored more than 5000 runs in the Ranji Trophy, came out of retirement to help Tamil Nadu to the 1987–8 championship, scoring 122 in the semi-final and 94 in the final.

V

Curiously enough, the founding family of Madras cricket was not Brahmin at all but hailed from the caste of Naidus. Its patriarch was M. Buchi Babu Naidu, one of the founders of the Madras United Club, formed after the exclusive Madras Cricket Club refused to admit non-Europeans. Buchi Babu, after whom a major tournament is named, also initiated the Presidency match between Indians and Europeans, played annually in Chepauk during the Pongal festival in early January.

While Buchi Babu died on the eve of the first Presidency match, three of his sons graced the fixture in later years. The eldest was a terrific hitter named Venkataramanujulu (Bhatt, for short). A second son, the elegant left-hander M. Baliah, known as the Madras Woolley, played for the Hindus in the Bombay Pentangular and for Madras in the first season of the Ranji Trophy, when he was forty-one. The next year, when C.P. Johnstone was unavailable, he captained Madras in a losing final against Bombay.

The most famous member of the Buchi Babu clan was Baliah's younger brother, C. Ramaswami, one of the two heroes with whom we began this book. When he went up to Cambridge, where he was C.P. Johnstone's contemporary, Ramaswami had already made his mark as a left-handed hitter in the Presidency matches. When he wasn't considered for the cricket trials at Cambridge, he turned to tennis, winning a Blue. On his return to India in 1924, he joined the Madras

Agricultural Service, and touring villages left him little time for tennis or cricket. He resumed active cricket only on being posted to Madras city in the early thirties. In the following years, his rivalry with the Anglo Indian hitter of the Europeans, Ren Nailer, was the set piece of the annual Presidency match. Pushing forty, Ramaswami top-scored (with 26!) in the first ever Ranji Trophy match, when Madras beat Mysore in a day. Next season, two innings of 48 not out and 82 for Madras against Jack Ryder's Australian team landed him a totally unexpected berth in the 1936 team to England. There, he made 40 and 60 on his Test debut in Manchester, his off-side driving drawing words of praise from Cardus himself.

In 1986, at the age of ninety Ramaswami walked out of his Madras home and was never seen again.* But he had lived long enough to see at least three nephews and one grandnephew play for the state. Two were sons of Venkataramanujulu, M.V. Prakash and M.V. Bobjee, the latter like his uncle a champion lawn tennis player. Baliah's son, M. Suryanarayana, was good enough to play an unofficial 'Test' as a middle-order batsman, while his innings of 31 and 47 helped Madras narrowly beat Holkar in the Ranji final of 1954–5. Closest to Ramaswami in batting style was Baliah's grandson, P. Ramesh, a left-handed hitter who played for Tamil Nadu in the nineteen-seventies.

VI

If Madras cricket's founding family was non-Brahmin, its first family has been, of all things, Sikh. Indeed, the Tamil speaking sardar, A.G. Ram Singh, has claims to being the greatest

---

* A correspondent in *The Cricketer* of March 1990 claimed on the authority of C.R. Rangachari that Ramaswami had a disagreement with his family and moved to an ashram, where he still lives. If he is alive, Cota Ramaswami would be the oldest living Test cricketer in the world.

cricketer to play for the state. Sadly, Ram Singh did not play a Test match, for his career overlapped with that of Vinoo Mankad, who did the same things, only a bit better—though, unlike the Sikh, Vinoo batted right handed. A pugnacious left-handed batsman, Ram Singh's best strokes were behind the wicket: the cut, the hook, and a short-arm pull he made his very own. As a left-arm spinner Ram Singh was only marginally inferior to the imperishable Mankad. It was said of him, as of other left armers before and since, that Ram Singh could drop the ball on a coin, so good was his control.

Despite the strong backing of C.P. Johnstone, Ram Singh was surprisingly not selected for the 1936 tour of England, although Mankad had not yet arrived on the scene. Several Madras critics felt that the Sikh should have been selected ahead of the forty-year-old Ramaswami, and so did Ramaswami himself. Ten years later, Ram Singh was again on the short list for the 1946 tour. As he recalls, 'Pataudi (senior) even asked me to keep my passport ready. But I was not destined to go. I was batting well in the selection match when I called for some water. The cold water brought on cramps and I was forced to retire. A prominent Indian cricketer spread the canard that I had a heart problem', and Ram Singh was not chosen.*

But nothing can take away Ram Singh's place in the annals of Madras cricket. He does not appear to have played in the Bombay Pentangular (at least two other Sikhs, Lall Singh and the Yuvraj of Patiala, did play for the Hindus), but he dominated the Madras Presidency matches. He is the only Indian to have scored two centuries in these games, while against his name are the best bowling figures for either side. A fairly typical performance came in the Presidency match of 1936—i.e. in the year he wasn't chosen for the England tour. Batting at

---

* Quoted in Suresh Menon, 'A family affair', *Express Magazine*, 30 July 1989.

number 3, he top-scored with 70, and then had figures of 9.3/ 3/14/8 and 12/0/34/5 in his side's innings victory over the Europeans.

Ram Singh's Ranji Trophy record is equally noteworthy. In that inaugural match, his match figures of 11 for 35 were instrumental in the one day victory over Mysore. He played twenty-seven Ranji Trophy matches without a break, spread over fourteen seasons. He was the second cricketer, after the legendary Amar Singh of Nawanagar, to complete the double of 1000 runs and 100 wickets in the championship. It is puzzling, to say the least, that he played only two unofficial 'Tests' for India: one apiece against Ryder's team (at Chepauk) and Lord Tennyson's M.C.C. side of 1937–8. In the first match he bowled only four overs, though he did take a wicked skier at deep extra-cover to dismiss Charlie Macartney.

Ram Singh won some consolation when two of his sons, A.G. Kripal Singh and A.G. Milkha Singh, played Test cricket. Modelling his game on Vijay Manjrekar's, Kripal made a stunning entry into Test cricket with an unbeaten hundred against New Zealand in 1955. This innings was beautifully timed, for this was the twenty-fifth anniversary of the Madras Cricket Association, and the Silver Jubilee Souvenir could now place, on its inside front cover, a full-page photograph of the hero of the moment.*

But Madras had other reasons to be grateful to Kripal

---

* The text of this advertisement, paid for by the leading Madras photographers, Klein and Peyerel, read: 'Our felicitations to A.G. Kripal Singh for his century on test debut, joining the ranks of K.S. Duleepsinhji, Nawab of Pataudi, Lala Amarnath and Deepak Shodhan'. I am still trying to unravel this message. The juxtaposition of two Indians who played for England with Amarnath and Shodhan may be explained by the fact that the Tamilians are as Anglophilic as the Bengalis, but in that case, why not add to the list the name of K.S. Ranjitsinhji, likewise a centurion on his Test debut? Or is it that Ranji is too holy a name to be mentioned in the same breath as the others, just as the Iyengar deity Vishnu must only be worshipped on his own, never with other members of the Hindu trinity?

Singh. In the preceding year, he had played in the first Madras team to win the Ranji Trophy. In what was very much a team effort, the left-arm spin of M.K. Murugesh, the batting of C.D. Gopinath (a fine off-side player capped eight times for India), and the leadership of Balu Alaganan all played their part. But Kripal Singh was the undoubted star of the Ranji final against Holkar—which Madras won by a mere 46 runs—with knocks of 75 and 91 and seven wickets in the match.

As an all-rounder, Kripal was good enough to be picked for India on the strength of his off-spinning prowess alone. Although he played fourteen Tests in all, spread over seven series, he never recaptured the high point of his debut. Tragically, Kripal died of a heart attack shortly after he turned fifty. But there is one record no one can take away from him. Converting to Christianity after marriage, Kripal is surely the only player to have played Test cricket under more than one religious affiliation.

His contemporaries remember Kripal best in turban and beard, while I can recall him only in his clean-shaven Christian years. His younger brother Milkha played four Tests against three countries, all in his turban. (He and Kripal played one Test together, against England in 1961–2.) Like his brother, he was capped for Madras before he turned eighteen. A fine hooker like his father, Milkha first came to notice as a member of the Indian Schoolboys, and made his Test debut when he was barely nineteen. The first to score a century in the Duleep Trophy, Milkha was one of the two Indian batsmen who always seemed to have the measure of the otherwise unstoppable duo of Prasanna and Chandrasekhar. (The other was Bombay's Ajit Wadekar, significantly also a left-hander.)

Another of Ram Singh's sons, A.G. Satwender Singh, also played for Indian Schoolboys and Madras, and but for a knee problem may well have played Test cricket. In the nineteen-sixties the three brothers all played league cricket in Madras, but for different teams: Kripal for E.I.D. Parry, Milkha for the State Bank of India, and Satwender for Alwarpet Cricket Club. Indeed, Ram Singh's family has showered its gifts abundantly on Madras cricket. Lately, the old man's nephew, A.G. Harjender Singh, and two of Kripal's sons, Swaran and Arjan, have played for Tamil Nadu, while I am told that Milkha's fourteen-year-old-son, like the father a turbaned left-hander, is a boy to watch for the future. In his debut season, Arjan Kripal Singh scored a triple hundred against Goa. More recently, he scored an infinitely more valuable century against the old enemy, Karnataka, a state which must by now be heartily sick of Ram Singh and his progeny.

The cricketing progress of the sons of Milkha and Kripal is being lovingly watched over by their grandfather, one of the country's leading coaches. Ironically, Ram Singh learnt the art of coaching from the Sussex and Nawanagar professional Bert Wensley, one of whose proteges was Vinoo Mankad. Ram Singh's own wards include C.D. Gopinath and several other members of the 1955 winning team. A soft-spoken man, Ram Singh's coaching style is very different from that of Lala Amarnath, the founding father of that other great cricketing family. Well into his sixties, Ram Singh would do the rounds of the city's schools on his scooter, a mode of transport that says much for the man's modesty and devotion to the game.

For the Tamilian, the stereotypical North Indian is a coarse, swearing Sardarji, while for every Sikh the stereotypical South India is an effete, *rasam*-eating Madrasi. It is therefore a delicious irony that a family of turbaned Sardars should be the most loved of Madras's cricketers. For their part, Ram Singh's family have tried hard to assimilate. Speaking flawless Tamil, they live (of course) in Triplicane, and prefer *idlis* and *sambaar* to their own fare of *sarson ka saag*. In fact, when one of Ram

Singh's sons moved to Delhi, he had to request a Madras friend to find him a house in the Tamil-dominated locality of Karol Bagh, for without an introduction his turban and beard would have been enough for the Tamil landlord to shut the door in his face.

This blending of Tamil culture with turbaned heads is best exemplified by their names, for Ram Singh and his sons are surely the only Sikhs with two initials before their given names. Apparently, when the left-arm spinner first came to Madras, the Tamilians asked him what his initials were. None, replied Ram Singh. That won't do, countered his hosts, and immediately set about equipping him with the kind of pedigree with which every South Indian is born. What is your ancestral village, they asked the all rounder. I am not sure, replied Ram Singh, but I would like to believe it is the holy city of Amritsar. And your family and caste name, demanded his relentless hosts. None, said the Sardar wistfully, but it does not matter, for I am a follower of the last Guru. So Amritsar Gurugobind Ram Singh he became, and then and only then did the Tamilians welcome him to their city.* (This story is true, but its sequel is probably apocryphal—namely that Kripal changed his name, but not his initials, on his conversion to Christianity, Amritsar Gurugobind metamorphosizing into Arnold George Kripal Singh!)

VII

I have always been interested in wicket-keepers, if only to the extent of wondering why any particular character would be such a glutton for punishment... The prophets of Baal who cut and gashed themselves with knives in

* I owe this story to Anand Doraswami of the *Deccan Herald*.

masochistic fury were sensible, even phlegmatic characters compared to the self-immolating souls who first took up wicket-keeping.

So wrote A.A. Thomson in a survey of the great English wicket-keepers called 'Stumpers of the World, Unite!'. Pitches may have vastly improved since the times Thomson was writing about, but wicket-keeping remains the most difficult job in the game. Not surprisingly, stumpers have always been sturdy characters, and so it has been in Madras. The first Indian stumper of note was in fact a Madrasi, K. Seshachar, with the left-armer P. Baloo one of the two men to emerge with credit from the England tour of 1911 by an All India side led by the Maharaja of Patiala.

Seshachar was (what else) an Iyengar, as were two of his more distinguished successors in Madras. One, S.V.T. Chari, kept wickets in an unofficial 'Test' and ended up as one of the city's leading surgeons. In keeping with his Brahmin upbringing, it was the Hobart Gold Medal—awarded for the best student in the Madras Medical College—that Chari considered to be the crowning achievement of his life, not his keeping for India, standing up to Mohammed Nissar. The man who followed him in the Madras team, M.O. Srinivasan, also played one unofficial 'Test', against the Australian Services side in 1945. Like his more famous contemporary, the Australian Don Tallon, Srinivasan was hard of hearing, relying on his slips to tell him when to appeal for a catch behind the wicket.

Following Srinivasan, the caste composition of Madras stumpers has been markedly diverse, validating Thomson's dictum that only the most intrepid characters, regardless of their social origins, would take up such a job. The keeper of the fifties was a Tamil Christian, D.L. Chakravarty, that of the sixties the portly P.K. Beliappa. Aptly nicknamed 'Belly', P.K.

was one of the very few top-flight cricketers from the tiny community of Coorgs that has produced hockey internationals and five-star generals by the sackful. In the seventies came along a Telugu speaker settled in Madras, Bharat Reddy. A successful captain of Indian Schoolboys, Reddy played for Rest of India and South Zone before he was selected for Tamil Nadu. Despite his sensational entry into big cricket, Reddy's elevation into the Test side was checked by the versatile Kirmani. Patiently awaiting his turn, Reddy acquitted himself most creditably when Kirmani was mysteriously dropped from the 1979 England tour (rumour had it that he was punished for flirting with Kerry Packer).

VIII

There can be little dispute about ten places in an all-time Madras/Tamil Nadu eleven. The only uncertainty regards the stumper, though I prefer Reddy to his gifted predecessors. Our eleven then reads

1. K. Srikkanth
2. C. Ramaswami
3. A.G. Milkha Singh
4. A.G. Kripal Singh
5. C.D. Gopinath
6. A.G. Ram Singh
7. M.J. Gopalan
8. Bharat Reddy (wicket-keeper)
9. S. Venkataraghavan (captain)
10. C. R. Rangachari
11. V.V. Kumar
Manager: S.K. Gurunathan

A word in conclusion about the institution that stands behind Madras cricket, *The Hindu*, otherwise known as the Mount Road Mahavishnu. The city's first inter-company tournament was endowed by the newspaper, being initially called the Sport and Pastime Trophy, and after the untimely demise of that fine weekly, The Hindu Trophy. Since 1947, it has ably documented *Indian Cricket* through the annual of that name started by the selfless S.K. Gurunathan, while in retaining Arthur Mailey, Jack Fingleton and Robin Marlar it has brought us the best in cricket writing. Two members of the family have been played for the state: the left-hand batsman K. Balaji, and N. Ram, who briefly kept wickets for Madras and is now helping to keep the nation's conscience.

CHAPTER SEVEN

Princely India : The Living

One of the most attractive things about the Ranji Trophy is its defiance, however partial, of the principle of linguistic states validated by the States Reorganization Committee of 1956. Thus the proponents of Samyukta (United) Maharashtra have been unable to do away with Bombay as a cricketing entity, while the Hyderabad Ranji Trophy team is clearly at odds with the philosophy of Vishaal (Greater) Andhra. And one Indian state, Gujarat, is broken up into no less than three cricket associations—Saurashtra, Baroda and Gujarat itself.

Saurashtra is a conglomeration of several Rajput princi-palities, the most famous among them being Ranji's Nawanagar, which I shall deal with in the next chapter. Baroda, which first entered the Ranji Trophy in 1937–8, is territorially speaking almost as it was before independence. In cricketing terms, at any rate, it is a relic of princely India which is quite alive. Indeed, it was Baroda which won the championship in the year before Bombay began its long, uninterrupted hold on the trophy.

II

The early decades of the Ranji Trophy were marked, as noted earlier, by a considerable circulation of cricketing elites. Maharashtra, Baroda and Holkar, in particular, participated in an active three-way exchange.*

The traffic was entirely in keeping with historical trends, for both Holkar and Baroda were chiefdoms founded by vassals of the great Maratha state of the Peshwas. The most famous of these Maratha exiles in Baroda was Vijay Samuel Hazare. Like G.R. Viswanath, to whom he is sometimes compared, Hazare was a most diffident genius: Dom Moraes once called him 'the man who hurries away if he hears himself being praised'. Hazare spent the war years compiling huge scores in the Bombay Pentangular and the Ranji Trophy, and was past thirty when he made his Test debut in England in 1946. Five years later, he led India to its first Test win, and the following year took his side on a memorable tour of the West Indies.

Hazare's best moments in Test cricket, however, were reserved for Australia. In the Sydney Test of 1947, a match India must surely have won but for rain, Hazare clean bowled Bradman with a sharp breakback for 13—the great man's only failure of the series. Then, in the Adelaide Test, he scored two immaculate hundreds against one of the finest ever Test attacks; a quarter century was to elapse before another Indian scored a century in each innings of a Test match. Keith Miller has related how Hazare, a marvellous on-side player, hit him repeatedly past square leg in this match, but to the bowler's disgust Bradman would not allow him an extra fieldsman on the leg-side. But Hazare's strokes were by no means restricted

---

* See P.N. Sundaresan and Anandji Dossa, editors, *Forty-five Years of Ranji Trophy: Volume 1: 1934–1959* (Board of Control for Cricket in India, 1980).

to one side of the wicket. In a report on his Adelaide centuries, Arthur Mailey was visibly impressed with Hazare's cover driving.

Miller, with his co-author R.S. Whittington, had also played against Hazare while touring India with the Australian Services side in 1945. Recalling that tour, Miller and Whittington said Hazare was 'as graceful as Archie Jackson'; a comparison no Australian would make lightly, for it is much like an Indian saying Steve Waugh is as elegant as G.R. Viswanath. Jackson, we may recall, was reckoned to be a better strokeplayer than his colleague Don Bradman. Dying at the age of twenty-three, he was for Miller and his generation the best-loved Australian cricketer after Victor Trumper.

Hazare did play several fine innings on his two tours of England. But, as John Arlott once wrote, he was a man 'much averse to walking in the rain': born and brought up on the sun-baked Deccan plateau, he must have been more at home in Australia. Long after he retired, Hazare was invited by the Lancashire Country Cricket Club for a function at Old Trafford. In his reply, Hazare dwelt on the rather wet and murky reputation of the Lancashire ground. Old Trafford, he remarked, 'seems to shine in the company of Jupiter Pluvius' (Jupiter, the rain god).*

So discomfited was Hazare by the Manchester gloom that in his match-saving innings of 44 in the Old Trafford Test of 1946 he hit the only six of his Test career; an act of desperation by one who was never known to lift the ball.

---

* Quoted in Tim Heald, *The Character of Cricket* (Faber and Faber, 1986), pp. 88–9.

III

For his adopted state of Baroda, Hazare's medium pace off-breaks (with a finger spun leg-break taught to him by Clarrie Grimmett) were as valuable as his unrivalled batting gifts. Vijay's younger brother Vivek (the brothers added over 300 for the ninth wicket in the Pentangular match in which Vijay scored 309 not out of his team's score of 387) also played many years for the state. More recently, the sons of Vijay and Vivek have played for Baroda. However, Vijay Hazare's most important bequest to Baroda cricket was his protege, Chandrakant Gulabrao 'Chandu' Borde.

Like his mentor, Borde was a Christian born in the southern Maharashtra town of Sangli. He studied at the Sangli High School, where he learnt to play under Hazare's own coach and the school's sportsmaster, Hanumant Rao Bhosle. (Hanumant Rao was the father of Vijay Bhosle, an attractive right-hand batsman who played for both Baroda and Bombay.) A critic on the 1959 England tour pointed to the uncanny similarities between the two, noting that Borde's drive off the back foot, and even his walk, were modelled on Hazare's. Borde was likewise a marvellous player of fast bowling, scoring three of his five Test hundreds against the West Indies—including a memorable double of 109 and 96 in the Delhi Test of 1958, when he hit his wicket while attempting to hook Gilchrist in the second innings. Fittingly, the only Test in which Borde captained India was in Adelaide, the ground where Hazare had hit his two centuries thirty years earlier.

Like his hero Borde was an all-rounder of prodigious gifts, though unlike him Borde bowled leg-breaks and googlies. Two of his opponents on that 1959 England tour, Trevor Bailey and Fred Trueman, favourably compared his bowling with Subhas Gupte's. With Gupte on the decline, Borde emerged as India's front-rank spinner, and, in combination with the left-armer Salim Durrani, bowled India to its first series win, against England in 1961–2. That winter, Borde tormented the England captain, Ted Dexter, thrice bowling him leg stump in the Test matches. Sadly, shoulder trouble forced Chandu to abandon bowling shortly afterwards, though he remained our leading Test batsman through much of the sixties.

Baroda has somehow had a great attraction for wrist-spinners. Of the foremost Indian exponents of this art in the era B.C. (Before Chandrasekhar), only the Gupte brothers, Subhas and Baloo, did not play for the state. C.S. Nayudu played one season for Baroda, while another Maharashtra exile, Sadashiv Shinde, stayed a while longer. More colourful than either was the rotund Amir Elahi. One of only three cricketers to play for both India and Pakistan, Elahi started out as a wicket-keeper opening batsman for Northern India and Southern Punjab. By the time he camped at Baroda in the mid-forties, he had already won considerable acclaim as the strike bowler for the Muslims in the Pentangular. He relished bowling, being known to laugh out loud on fooling the batsman. For Baroda he batted number eleven, but spearheaded his team's bowling in at least two winning Ranji campaigns.

Elahi was also on that 1947 tour of Australia, though in his only Test appearance in the rain-affected match at Sydney he did not bowl a ball. Three other Baroda cricketers in that hapless Indian team were all batsman: G. Kishenchand, H.R. Adhikari, and Gul Mahommed. A Sindhi from Karachi, Kishenchand played more than twenty seasons for Baroda. He will go down in cricketing history as the bowler off whom Don Bradman scored the hundredth run of his hundredth hundred. Before joining the Army, Hemu Adhikari had spent his formative cricketing years in Baroda. A brilliant cover field and combative batsman, Adhikari played Test cricket with some success in three continents. In that Adelaide Test, he added 130 with Hazare, enabling his Baroda teammate to score his second century of the match. He is probably better known to the younger generation as a martinet among coaches and managers: he managed the Indian team on the England tours of 1971 and 1974, and was, for a number of years, national cricket coach. Gul Mahommed, who, like Amir Elahi, went on to play for Pakistan after Partition, was a marvellous fielder with the priceless gift (for a cover point) of being left-handed. A stylish batsman, like other left-handers he was especially strong in the area between backward point and extra cover.

IV

So much for the commoners of Baroda cricket. We now come to the state's ruling family, eight of whose members played first-class cricket (and, truth be told, at least six were cricketers). Among these were the Maharaja's younger brother S.P. Gaekwad, and his uncle, J.M. Ghorpade. A fine opening batsman who once captained Combined Universities, Sangram Gaekwad only narrowly missed Test selection. 'Mama' Ghorpade was luckier, playing Test cricket against four countries in the nineteen-fifties. Ghorpade, who was at one time a serious contender for the India captaincy, was something of a bits-and-pieces cricketer; middle-order bat, fine field, and part-time leg-spinner.

Two of the ruler's more distant kinsmen were D.K. Gaekwad and his son Anshuman. When Hemu Adhikari, by any reckoning, should have been selected as captain for the 1959 England tour, D.K. Gaekwad was the surprise choice. After India lost that series five-nil, Gaekwad must have felt very much like the England bowler Fred Tate, who after a historic failure in his only Test is reported to have said: 'I have a son at home

(Maurice Tate) who shall make up for it one day'. Indeed, Dattaji's son, Anshuman, emerged in due course as one of the most courageous batsmen of modern times. In two successive series he took a fearful pounding from Andy Roberts, Michael Holding and company, but never once flinched. Twenty-two years after his debut for the state as a schoolboy off-spinner, Anshuman is still playing for Baroda in the Ranji Trophy.

We come finally to the Maharaja himself, His Highness Fatehsinghrao Gaekwad of Baroda ('Jackie' to his friends and intimates). When Baroda last won the Ranji Trophy, in 1957–8, no less than five members of the winning side were employed by the Maharaja. Borde and Kishenchand were listed simply as being 'on the staff of H.H.Baroda', while his kinsmen D.K. Gaekwad and J.M. Ghorpade, and the great Hazare, were in the more elevated position of being ADCs to the ruler. For long an influential member of India's cricket establishment, Fatehsinghrao Gaekwad had served as President of the Board of Control for Cricket in India, and as manager of Indian touring sides in England and Pakistan.

But Fatehsinghrao was not just a patron of cricket. An attractive batsman, he made his first-class debut for Baroda as a schoolboy of sixteen, and in the years that followed he played for the state when his duties allowed. When Hazare and Gul Mahommed had their world record stand of 577 for the fourth wicket, in the 1946–7 final against Holkar, the Maharaja, as next man in, also set a world record of sorts by being padded up for two and a half days. When he finally got to bat, C.K. Nayudu dismissed him for one.

Eleven years later, in the winter of Baroda's last triumph, Fatehsinghrao did not play in the early matches, but when his team entered the final he dusted his flannels and came out of retirement. Till then, Baroda had played their home engagements on a matting wicket at the Coronation Gymkhana

BARODA'S BATTING BASTION

*Motibagh Palace Grounds ... Three o'clock in the afternoon ...
V.S. Hazare—120 not out*

ground, but for the final, against a Services side captained by the Baroda exile Hemu Adhikari, they shifted to a newly-laid turf wicket at the Maharaja's own Motibagh Palace.

The match itself was dominated by the forty-two-year-old Hazare. That master strategist, Hemu Adhikari, knew that for his team to have any chance they would have to get Hazare out quickly. After being hit by the England fast bowler, Fred Ridgway, in a Test match in the early fifties, Hazare had developed the shadow of a weakness against the bouncer. Hemu was aware of this, and, after Baroda had lost an early wicket, instructed his eager young fast bowler, Surendranath, to bowl a bumper first ball at the master. Sure enough, Hazare hooked in the air, but deep fine leg spilled the catch. 'Now he'll get a hundred', exclaimed an exasperated Adhikari. In fact, Hazare got not one hundred but two, and, with 203 and six cheap wickets, was the undoubted match-winner. In his one innings, Fatehsinghrao scored only nine runs batting at number six. Nonetheless, he will go down in history as the only Maharaja to play as a sitting Member of Parliament for a victorious side in a Ranji Trophy final, and that, moreover, on a ground owned and maintained by himself.

V

Baroda's sole representative in the national side now is the pesky wicket-keeper Kiran More, whose exubérance—he must be the loudest appealer in the game today—is tempered at home by the sage presence of Anshuman Gaekwad at first slip. (Prior to More, another Test keeper from Baroda was R.B. Nimbalkar, who toured England in 1946.) Nor must we forget the stylish left-hander Deepak Shodhan, a centurion on his Test debut who, after many years with Gujarat moved to Baroda. An all-time Baroda XI, just a bit short in bowling but

139

with extraordinary depth in batting would then read:

1. A.D. Gaekwad
2. D.K. Gaekwad
3. V.S. Hazare (captain)
4. C.G. Borde
5. D.H. Shodhan
6. H.R. Adhikari
7. G. Kishenchand
8. Gul Mahommed
9. J.M. Ghorpade
10. Kiran More (wicket-keeper)
11. Amir Elahi

In these democratic times, the twelfth man can be Fatehsinghrao himself.

VI

Three years after Baroda's victory over the Services at the Motibagh Palace, Rajasthan entered the Ranji Trophy final for the first time. Rajasthan cricket was guided at the time by His Highness Bhagwatsinghji of Mewar, the Maharana of Udaipur, known reverentially as Hinduva-Suraj (The Sun of the Hindus). Udaipur, of course, was very much *primus inter pares* in the Rajput principalities of the desert which came together to form the state of Rajasthan after Independence. And with the princes of Jodhpur and Jaipur preferring to patronize polo, Bhagwatsingh could play as strikingly similar a role for his Ranji Trophy side as Fatehsinghrao did in his.

Indeed, the resemblance is quite uncanny. For example, in 1958 Dicky Rutnagur's *Indian Cricket Field Annual* lists the following Rajasthan cricketers as being on the staff of H.H.

Mewar (Bhagwatsinghji's abbreviated title): the batsman B.B. Nimbalkar (formerly of Maharashtra, Holkar and Baroda, and shortly to move to the Railways); the leg-spinner C.G. Joshi; and three left-handed all-rounders—Arjun Naidu, Ramesh Shah, and the one and only Salim Durrani. And, like the Gaekwad of Baroda, Bhagwatsingh was no more patron, for he opened Rajasthan's batting for many years.

Bhagwatsingh's dearest wish, of course, was to emulate the ruler of Baroda by playing in a Ranji Trophy winning side. He took a vow that if Rajasthan ever won the championship, he would take a dip in the holy Ganga. So, when Rajasthan entered the final of 1960–1, he made sure of hosting it in his home town of Udaipur. The parallels with Baroda end there, for, despite the presence of several Test cricketers imported from Bombay, Rajasthan lost to the island city by seven wickets.

That defeat at the Bhopal Nobles' College ground in Udaipur began a run of four years in which Rajasthan were defeated in successive finals by Bombay. In all, Rajasthan lost seven finals to Bombay in the nineteen-sixties. Tragically, Rajasthan faded away just as Bombay began to lose its hold on the Ranji Trophy, and in its last final, 1973–4, it caved in meekly to Karnataka.

VII

When Dilip Vengsarkar was having a particularly difficult time at Bombay, Rajasthan offered him the captaincy of their own side as a springboard for the Indian captaincy. (Vengsarkar did not move when Bombay changed its mind about not appointing him their captain.) In this they were continuing a long tradition of welcoming former Bombay players, for Mankad, Gupte, Ramchand and Manjrekar—to name only four international stars—ended their playing days with Rajasthan.

Meanwhile, Bhagwatsingh induced several younger cricketers to come and make Rajasthan their home. These included the left-handed K.M. Rungta, who first played for Maharashtra; the wrist-spinner C.G. Joshi, formerly of Gujarat; and the fast bowlers G.R. Sunderam and Kailash Gattani, both of whom first learnt the game in Bombay.

But like the present English Test team, Rajasthan was not *merely* a side of immigrants. In time, the Rajput rulers unbent enough to allow their sons to play what was hitherto considered—in comparison to polo and pigsticking—a soft and unmanly game. One such prince was Raj Singh Dungarpur, the medium pace bowler who is presently the grey eminence of Indian cricket. A second was the fine opening batsman and wicket-keeper, and heir to the throne of Banswara, Suryaveer Singh. Standing above them both was Suryaveer's younger brother, Hanumant Singh. Prince among batsmen and gentleman among cricketers, Hanumant, who hit a cultured hundred on his Test debut, deserved to play for India far longer than he did.

Meanwhile, a great teacher had moved to Rajasthan's capital, Jaipur. This was N.D. Marshall, the first Indian instructor for cricket coaches at the National Institute for Sports. Marshall had toured England as an opening batsman in 1932. As a coach he was equalled only by Lala Amarnath in his knowledge of the game and in the terror he exercised, primarily through an acerbic tongue, over his pupils. One of his proteges in Jaipur was the hard-hitting wicket-keeper-batsman Sunil Benjamin. A second was the opening batsman Laxman Singh, a member of that remarkable Indian Schoolboys team of 1967–8. (When Laxman died following a fall at the young age of forty, his former schoolboy captain, Surinder Amarnath, was by his side). A third was Parthasarthy Sharma, whose masterful knocks of 54 and 49 (run out) on his debut against the West Indies appear to signal the start of a long Test career. Unfortunately he acquired a name (deserved) for being slow in the field, and another (largely undeserved) for being a poor runner between the wickets, and in the end played only five Tests.

VIII

The pride of Rajasthan cricket in its glorious phase, however, was that wayward genius Salim Durrani, the only man between Vinoo Mankad and Kapil Dev to win Test matches for India with both bat and ball. Born in Kabul, Salim learnt the game at Jamnagar, where his father Abdul Aziz ran a cricket school. He made his first-class debut as a schoolboy wicket-keeper for Saurashtra, and then played one season for Gujarat. He had therefore moved considerably around the west coast before Bhagwatsingh coaxed him to Rajasthan.

Durrani came to a state he quickly made his own as a wicket-keeper and strokeful left-hand batsman. In 1958–9 he kept wickets for Central Zone against the West Indies, scoring 80 at number four. Yet, three winters later, Durrani was India's leading bowler in her first series victory against England: surely one of the most amazing transformations in the history of the game.

It was Vinoo Mankad who encouraged Durrani to take up bowling, and then taught him the craft of left-arm spin. The pupil had a classical high action, sharp turn, and, like the master himself, a deadly armer. Ten years after his first bowling triumphs, Durrani dismissed Clive Lloyd and Gary Sobers in one over to help win the 1971 Port of Spain Test. On an earlier visit to the Caribbean, India had been thrashed five-nil, but Durrani had one unforgettable moment, again at Port of Spain. With India facing their fourth successive defeat, Durrani was down to bat at number nine in the second innings. But he defied the captain (the twenty-one-year-old Pataudi) and hijacked the batting, coming in first wicket down. Flaying Hall, Sobers and Gibbs to all parts of the Queens Park Oval, Durrani scored his only century in Test cricket.

My favourite Durrani story relates to his last series as an international player, against England in 1972–3. With the spin quartet in their prime, Durrani was playing as a batsman. In the low-scoring Madras Test, Salim's two innings of 38 apiece were decisive. When England were batting in that match, Bedi temporarily left the field, and Wadekar threw the ball to Durrani, that other great left-armer. It was crisply returned to the captain, with the words, 'main change bowler nahin hoon' (I am not a change bowler).

The adjectives most favoured by sportswriters in describing Durrani were 'wayward', 'impetuous', 'mercurial', and 'temperamental', epithets which no doubt influenced the selectors. To be sure, he was all of these things, but he was also a magnificent cricketer. Durrani's own lasting regret was that he was never picked for a tour of England, although India made three visits there during his career. Known in the dressing rooms simply as 'Prince Salim', he was a cricketer much admired by his peers, if the autobiographies of those two judicious men, Prasanna and Gavaskar, are anything to go by. This admiration was quite evident when I saw him play in a benefit match in Delhi several years after he had played his last Test. The nawabs of Hyderabad notwithstanding, Durrani was surely the handsomest Indian to play big cricket, and he even acted, purely on the basis of his looks, in a Hindi feature film. He cut a fine figure as he walked out to bat that day at the Kotla, his tall and angular appearance sharpened by his idiosyncratic habit of buckling his pads on the inside of his legs. In his last Test series, Durrani had become famous for hitting sixes (off the English left-armers Gifford and Underwood) on request, and clearly he was expected to do so this time too. The bowler, Bishen Bedi, gave his three cheers, and tossed up a slow half volley. Salim swung, got a top edge, and Surinder Amarnath ran round in circles at mid-wicket in a largely convincing bid to fool the crowd that he had misjudged the skier. To the next ball, Salim swung again, and the ball went soaring towards long-on. It actually landed just inside the boundary, but a six was signalled—with Bedi leading the applause—and the crowd was content.

IX

In his demeanour and cricketing style, Durrani was more of a prince than the blue-blooded Rajput chiefs who also played for the state. He exemplified the cavalier spirit of Rajasthan cricket, a spirit that contrasts so sharply with the professionalism of Bombay, and which perhaps explains the string of defeats in the Ranji final. This spirit was also embodied in Durrani's spin twin for Rajasthan, C.G. 'Chandu' Joshi.

Even as Durrani emerged as a left-arm spinner under the guidance of Vinoo Mankad, Joshi came of age as a leg-break bowler while fielding at slip to Rajasthan's other legendary Bombay exile, Subhas Gupte. Curiously, Joshi shared his initials and first name with Durrani's spinning partner for India, C.G. Borde. Their bowling styles were also quite similar. Both the Chandus relied more on flight than on turn, and were slower through the air than most modern leg-spinners— closer, shall we say, to Mushtaq Mohammed than to Abdul Qadir.

For a living, Chandu Joshi taught art and sculpture at that reputed public school in Ajmer, Mayo College. One can readily appreciate that leg-spinners would make fine artists, just as fast

145

bowlers make effective policemen. (One of the most celebrated of the tribe, Arthur Mailey, was a cartoonist by profession. Accused by his fellow Australians of passing on trade secrets to England's googly bowler, Ian Peebles, Mailey contemptuously replied: 'Spin bowling is an art. And art is international'.) Anyway, it is not clear whether Joshi cultivated artistic skills in his wards, but he did mould a generation of fine cricketers, including at least one future Test batsman. Chandu was the solitary example in Indian cricket of a phenomenon quite familiar in the history of English cricket: the schoolmaster who, in the holidays, comes straight out of the classroom to take his rightful place among the elect of the game. Joshi must also have retired from first-class cricket more often than any other Indian. Each time he called it a day, a desperate message from Rajasthan's captain, Hanumant Singh, would follow him to Ajmer: 'Very short of bowlers. Please report to Jaipur for Ranji Trophy match against. . . .Last chance to win championship'. It was a call the little leg-spinner could scarcely resist (and it came from one of the most charming of cricketers), and with a word of explanation to the Mayo College Principal, he would be on his way.

Like all spin bowlers, Chandu Joshi abhorred plumb wickets. Confronted with one, he would mutter in disgust: '*Kanna neep nahin, kanna neep nahin*' (there is no nip in this wretched wicket). Again, like all slow bowlers, he relished his triumphs to the last. Pushing fifty, he brought a team of schoolboys to play my college in Delhi. Then, on a plumb wicket with no nip, he bowled us out with a marvellous exhibition of spin bowling, his victims including three of his former Mayo College pupils then playing for St Stephen's. Each wicket was followed by a brief peroration, comparing it to some success in bygone days. Thus, when a left-hander was caught in the leg trap, he was told as he departed: 'That was how I got

146

Surinder Amarnath, Duleep Trophy semi-final, 1971'. And a right-hander caught at slip, cutting at a googly, was duly informed: 'Aah! Just like G.R. Viswanath, Ranji Trophy final, 1974'.

X

If we restrict our all-time Rajasthan XI to those who were either born or domiciled in the state, thereby taking out of consideration the Bombay professionals, it should read:

1. Suryaveer Singh
2. Laxman Singh
3. Hanumant Singh (captain)
4. P. Sharma
5. S.A. Durrani
6. K.M. Rungta
7. Sunil Benjamin (wicket-keeper)
8. Kailash Gattani
9. H.H. Mewar
10. G.R. Sunderam
11. C.G. Joshi

Unlike Fatehsinghrao Gaekwad, thwarted by the abundant batting talent in Baroda, Bhagwatsingh may just sneak into the all-time XI of his state; some consolation for failing to win the Ranji Trophy on his home ground. However, although Banswara was a chiefdom small in size and influence compared with Udaipur, and Hanumant is but a younger son, it is he, and not the Sun of the Hindus, who shall be captain here.

CHAPTER EIGHT

Princely India : A Requiem

Fear has been an inseparable companion of most of our post-war cricketers—fear of getting hurt, or losing one's wicket, or one's reputation, or losing the match.

C.K. Nayudu, 1964

*T*here can be no doubt, I think, that C.K. Nayudu was the most remarkable character in the history of Indian cricket. His role in the development of the game in this country is equivalent to that of W.G. Grace in England, Don Bradman in Australia, or Learie Constantine in the West Indies. When *Indian Cricket* chose him one of their cricketers of the year in 1951—eighteen years after Wisden had selected him as one of their five cricketers of the year—the almanac's editor, S.K. Gurunathan, said simply that in 'honouring C.K. Nayudu, Indian cricket honours itself'.

C.K.'s father and uncle were friends of Ranjitsinhji at Cambridge. The only piece of coaching Nayudu ever received was relayed to him via his uncle by Ranji. This consisted of three crisp bits of advice: '*Balla Seedha Rakho. Jore Se Maro. Ghabrao Mat.*' (Keep a straight bat. Hit hard. And don't be afraid.) Although he did occasionally hit against the turn, in the main C.K. followed these three axioms. An attacking batsman who

148

founded his game on the drive, both lofted and along the ground, Nayudu was also, in Scyld Berry's words, 'a candidate for being considered the toughest cricketer between "W.G." and Brian Close, (Berry writes as an Englishman, but there is reason to believe that C.K. was in fact tougher than either.) C.K. has gone down in cricketing folklore as a great hitter, but his all round abilities were considerable. C.B. Fry even compared Nayudu's bowling to that of the legendary Australian Hugh Trumble, likewise a medium paced off-spinner with a puzzling flight. And watching C.K. field, Jack Hobbs remarked: 'You only have to see him pick up a ball to know that he is a born cricketer.' *

C.K.'s claims to greatness, of course, do not rest on his cricketing genius alone. His longevity, for example, is truly mind-boggling, for he had a career at the highest level that stretched further than that of W.G. Grace, Jack Hobbs, or Wilfred Rhodes. In 1916, at the age of twenty-one, he made his debut as a medium pace bowler and attacking number eight batsman for the Hindus in the Bombay Quadrangular. (The Rest had not yet arrived to make this a five cornered competition.) In 1926, by now his team's lynchpin, C.K. played the first great innings by an Indian against an international side. This was his brilliant 153 (11 sixes and 13 fours) for the Hindus against A.E.R. Gilligan's M.C.C. side, an innings lovingly described by E.L. Docker in his *History of Indian Cricket.* Ten years later, and at the age of forty-one, Nayudu played his last international series, in England, making his highest Test score in the third Test at the Oval. In 1946, having just crossed fifty, C.K. was chief selector of the Indian team which toured England that summer. In March 1946, just prior to that

---

* See 'Eskari (B. Sarbadhikari), *C. K. Nayudu* (Illustrated News, Calcutta, 1945); Vasant Raiji, *C. K. Nayudu: The Shahenshah of Indian Cricket* (Marine Sports, Bombay, 1989).

Nayudu's sixth six—over square leg and into the Plaza Cinema

England tour, Nayudu scored a match-winning 200 (in six and a half hours, with 22 fours) for Holkar in the Ranji Trophy final, and this against a Baroda attack which included three Test bowlers.

Ten years after that innings, C.K. made his final bow in first-class cricket at the age of sixty-one. Holkar had now disbanded, and he captained Uttar Pradesh against a Rajasthan attack which included Vinoo Mankad. The subsequent events have been described by one who played in that match, Raj Singh:

> The Old Man came in when his side had lost four cheap wickets and Vinoo Mankad was bowling. Now there had always been rivalry between them. It was Vinoo who suggested to Phadkar that he bowl the bouncer which hit C.K. in the mouth. And in 1952 Mankad had been refused a tour guarantee by C.K., then chairman of selectors, which resulted in Mankad not being a member of the touring party to England. Vinoo's first ball to the Old Man came in with the arm and had him absolutely plumb leg-before, except that the umpire wouldn't give him out. Second ball Vinoo was so furious that he bowled a beamer which nearly took the Old Man's head off and went for four byes. Third ball he pitched up and C.K. swung him away for six; Vinoo just stood there and glared, and the Old Man stood there too, his back ramrod straight as it was until the end of his life. Fourth ball C.K. again swung him away for six, another seven-iron shot. He made 84 that day before he was run out, after he had dropped his bat going for a third run.*

* Raj Singh, quoted in Scyld Berry, *Cricket Wallah* (Hodder and Stoughton, 1982), p. 149.

That C.K. could retain his batting skills after forty years of first-class cricket must be explained above all by his courage: '*Ghabrao Mat*' (don't be afraid) is the injunction he seems to have taken most to heart. In his last Test innings, he was hit over the heart by a bouncer from the England captain, Gubby Allen, and sank to his knees with a sigh that could be heard all over the ground. Rising to his feet, he stiffly waved off help, rushed out to the next delivery, and hit it to mid-wicket for four. He went on to make 81 in an unavailing bid to save the match. Sixteen years later, at the age of fifty-seven, C.K. led Holkar into a Ranji final against Bombay. Early on in his innings, he was struck in the mouth by a bumper from Dattu Phadkar—as Raj Singh has suggested, it may have been Vinoo Mankad who urged Phadkar to bounce the Old Man. Impatiently sweeping away three front teeth from the pitch, he resumed batting. Phadkar, out of respect for Nayudu, cut down his pace. 'Dattu', C.K. rebuked him sternly, 'do not let up. I am fine'. Nayudu went on to score 60 against an attack which contained no less than *six* Test bowlers—Phadkar, Sohoni, Ramchand, Mankad, Gupte and Shinde.

His courage on the field was matched by his courage off it, for C.K. was the first Indian cricketer to stand up for his just deserts. In a deferential age when princes ruled Indian cricket on and off the field, Nayudu insisted on his rights as the foremost Indian cricketer. When the Cricket Board pushed the Nawab of Pataudi (senior) as the unanimous choice for the 1936 England tour, Nayudu rightly called for an election, which he then unsuccessfully contested. After Pataudi withdrew, the Board wanted the Maharajkumar of Vizianagaram—a princely patron but indifferent cricketer—to replace him. Nayudu contested again, but 'Vizzy', by promising different state associations representation in the touring side in return for their vote, managed to win. Again, after leading Central

India in their first Ranji Trophy match, C.K. was replaced as captain by a minor prince, the Maharajkumar of Alirajpur. Nayudu withdrew from the team and did not play in the championship for the next five years, returning only in the nineteen-forties as captain of the newly formed Holkar side.

His courage (both physical and moral), longevity and playing skills all made C.K. a hero to a whole generation of Indian cricketers. When he was appointed captain for India's first Test series at home, one of his first acts was to send a telegram to D.R. Jardine and his team abroad the S.S. Mooltan— 'Wait till you see me'. In fact Jardine's men saw him everywhere, for with C.K.'s crowd appeal, he was made to play for all sorts of local sides against the M.C.C., and in all played a dozen times against the visitors. Jardine was so fed up that he called his opponents 'C.K. Nayudu's roving circus'. (In fairness to C.K. one must point out here that, unlike the M.C.C., which travelled comfortably in the first class, C.K. travelled second class.) But Nayudu's presence was required not merely as an attraction for spectators. Thus his appearance for the Punjab Governor's XI against the tourists was closely watched by the young North Zone all-rounder, Prithviraj, who was due to play against Jardine's team in the next match at Lahore. C.K.'s brilliant hitting, recalled Prithviraj, 'had driven away all fear of the foreigner from my mind'.

But like W.G. himself, C.K.'s forbidding exterior concealed a soft heart. The writer Bernard Hollowood has related how he was persuaded by his Indian friend, a Dr Bhandarkar (perhaps a member of the distinguished Indore family which spawned the wicket-keeper and coach Kamal Bhandarkar) that C.K. would welcome a visit on the night before the Oval Test of 1936. After dining well, they knocked on C.K.'s hotel room around midnight. Before them, 'in his nightshirt and rubbing sleep from his eyes was the unhappy Nayudu'. C.K. was 'courtesy itself' as the 'doctor mumbled something about mutual acquaintances', but 'when he batted, later on the same day, he did so like a man who had been kept awake half the night by a couple of unfeeling rogues. He made 5 and it is conceivable that his failure cost India the match.' After a 'decent rest', goes on Hollowood, Nayudu 'made 81 in the second innings, and we watched this knock enveloped in shame at the enormity of our behaviour'.

There is no more decisive triumph in cricket than hitting the ball over the boundary, and perhaps C.K.'s reputation as a hitter of sixes symbolized public appreciation of his longstanding battles against English cricketers, autocratic princes, and Anno Domini. Just as every district in India takes pride in a legendary visit of Rama and Sita, so every cricket ground has a story of a famous six hit out of its premises by C.K. Nayudu. Playing in the old RSI ground in Bangalore, C.K. is reputed to have struck a ball, off the Mysore fast bowler, across the adjoining Cubbon Road into Baird's Barracks beyond—a carry of over 120 yards. Batting in the Garden City on another occasion, this time at the Central College ground, Nayudu hit a straight six, off the back foot, into the compound of Swastik Talkies. Nayudu seemed to have cinema houses in his sights, for, in one of the early Moin-ud-Dowlah matches in Secunderabad, he lofted a ball out of the Gymkhana ground and into the premises of the Plaza Cinema. And as for a six he hit at Lord's in 1932, a critic wrote merely that 'the ball was last seen sailing in an easterly direction'.

II

In an era of shifting allegiances and porous boundaries, C.K. played for no less than four different teams in the Ranji Trophy, although by the time the championship began he was already forty. Ending as captain of Uttar Pradesh, he was the first captain of Central India, the first captain and founder vice-president of the Holkar Cricket Association, and the first captain and founder president of the Andhra Pradesh Cricket Association. (The only comparison one can make here is with Ho Chi Minh, founder member of four national communist parties, and founder chairman of two.) His best days, however, were reserved for Holkar, whom he led to four victories in eight years. The Maharaja of Holkar, Yeshwant Rao, once remarked: 'I may be the ruler of the state, but C.K. is surely the King of Outdoor Games'. True to the Maharaja's word, C.K. was left in complete control of Holkar cricket.

In Indore itself, C.K. could call upon a wide range of talent. He began with Ishtiaq Ali and his more famous brother, Mushtaq Ali. Mushtaq was in many ways the master's favourite pupil, so much so that 'Balla Seedha Rakho' (keep a straight bat) was a piece of advice C.K. allowed him to forget. Indisputably the most stylish Indian batsman between K.S. Ranjitsinhji and G.R. Viswanath, Mushtaq, like the Hyderabad nawabs, dressed as smartly as he batted; indeed, he was known to send his cricket shirt for ironing during the lunch interval of an important match. He was a particular favourite of the Calcutta crowd, who twice threatened to stop an international match when Mushtaq was not picked for the home side.

Although Salim Durrani has since emulated Mushtaq in being included in an Indian side on public demand, there is one distinction the Holkar stylist holds all on his own. He is, to date, the only Indian batsman to have been at the receiving end of a defamatory campaign directed at him by a visiting captain. On the Australian Services tour of 1945, Lindsay Hasset, hoping to give Mushtaq a complex, described him repeatedly as an 'ugly batsman'. Mushtaq got his own back when Hasset compiled a laborious century in one of the tour matches.

Observing the Australian's painful crawl, Mushtaq wryly told R.S. Whittington: 'Hasset, full of grace as usual'. Whittington himself had no illusions about Mushtaq's style, calling him the 'modern Ranji'.

Mushtaq's inseparable companion in Indore was the Old Man's younger brother C.S. Nayudu. Keith Miller, who played against him in 1945 and 1947, called C.S. 'the Indian whose cricket and personality I most admire'. A hard-hitting batsman and brilliant fieldsman, the younger Nayudu was known best for his abilities as a leg-break googly bowler. Like his brother, C.S. was both ageless—playing nearly thirty years of first class cricket—and tireless, setting a world record by bowling 917 balls in a first class match (64.5/10/153/6 and 88/12/275/5), the Ranji Trophy final of 1945 against Bombay. Very much like the Kent and England leg-spinner of the inter-war period, A.P. Freeman, C.S. had an indifferent Test record despite his success in domestic cricket. He only bowled upto his considerable abilities in one international series, against a visiting Commonwealth side, when he and another prodigious spinner, George Tribe, were the leading bowlers of their respective teams.

Three other home-grown products of that famous Holkar side were K.V. Bhandarkar, M.M. Jagdale and J.N. Bhaya. A fine wicket-keeper-batsman, in later years Bhandarkar moved to Poona, where he coached Chetan Chauhan, Yajuvendra Singh, and other future Test cricketers. M.M. Jagdale opened the bowling and batting; two of his sons, Ashok and Sanjay, played for many years in Holkar's successor side, Madhya Pradesh. The diminutive Bhaya was a middle-order batsman and part-time wicket-keeper, who, like Lall Singh, Gul Mahommed and a few others, was capped for India (in an unofficial 'Test') mainly on account of his fielding.

This reservoir of local talent was skilfully augmented by

C.K. From Maharashtra he attracted C.T. Sarwate, K.M. Rangnekar and B.B. Nimbalkar. A versatile all-rounder on the field and finger-print expert off it, Chandu Sarwate toured both England and Australia with the Indian team. In England he did not play a Test, but had one famous innings, when he and Shute Bannerjee, as numbers ten and eleven, both scored centuries in a last-wicket stand of 249 against Surrey. The next winter, after Mushtaq and Merchant had both opted out of the Australian tour, Sarwate was thrust into the most unenviable position then available in Test cricket: opening the batting against Ray Lindwall and Keith Miller. As a bowler Sarwate, like Sonny Ramadhin, mixed off-breaks and leg-breaks (he didn't bowl a googly). Khandu Rangnekar, who was also on that very difficult Australian tour, has claims to being the most attractive Indian left-hander ever (only Keki Mistri, whom Ranji once called the 'Clem Hill of the Parsis', would run him close in this regard). A cover specialist and former badminton champion, he too never fulfilled his promise in the Test arena. As for B.B. Nimbalkar, this prolific batsman never played a Test, but his 443 not out for Maharashtra against Kathiawar will remain the highest first class score on Indian soil. The Kathiawar side conceded the match with Nimbalkar just nine runs short of Bradman's then world record score of 452.

The three Maharashtrians were established cricketers when they moved to Holkar. By contrast, Hiralal Gaekwad, who like C.K. was born at Nagpur, was recruited after only one season with C.P. and Berar. The left arm 'Ghasu' Gaekwad was a holy terror on the mat, but he failed on his only overseas tour, of England in 1952. Perhaps this was because his powers of spin and cut were deadened by the slow English turf, but more likely he missed C.K.'s comforting presence at mid on. His devotion to the Old Man was total. A friend remembers Ghasu tying Nayudu's bootlaces and buckling his pads, in a match played by Holkar at Dehradun in the early fifties.

As for C.K.'s last recruit, here's the quiz question: who is the only Englishman to score an unbeaten double century in a Ranji Trophy final and yet end up on the losing side? None other than the great Denis Compton, who assisted Holkar while stationed near Indore during the Second World War.

On account of this astonishing diversity of talent and Nayudu's own towering presence, the Holkar team of the forties was arguably the most awesome side ever to play in the Ranji Trophy. In purely cricketing terms, various Bombay sides may have been better, man for man, but they never evoked the awe among other cricket teams that Nayudu and Holkar invariably did. When Holkar scored 912 for 8 declared against Mysore in 1945–6—a score that remains a record in the Ranji Trophy—the Mysore cricketers returned from Indore with terrifying stories of their ordeal in the field. A solitary humorist amongst them quipped: 'We ran so many times to the boundary and back. But if we had only run in a straight line from Indore to Bangalore, we would have saved our Cricket Association the railway fare.'

An all-time Holkar XI—if C.K. would allow anybody else to select one—should be as follows:

1. S. Mushtaq Ali
2. K.V. Bhandarkar (wicket-keeper)
3. C.K. Nayudu (captain)
4. D.C.S. Compton
5. K.M. Rangnekar
6. B.B. Nimbalkar
7. J.N. Bhaya
8. C.T. Sarwate
9. C.S. Nayudu
10. M.M. Jagdale

11. H.G. Gaekwad
12th man S. Ishtiaq Ali

Kamal Bhandarkar could conceivably be replaced by N.R. Nivsarkar, a leading Indore physician and the wicket-keeper of the championship team of the late forties.

As Mushtaq Ali and C.S. Nayudu will livingly testify, the elder Nayudu was a stern disciplinarian, but he was not unyielding. C.K. would certainly have been appalled by the modern habits of drinks being frequently carried for batsmen, and of fielders lounging on the ground at the fall of a wicket. In his time C.K. refused to allow his cricketers to take any liquid refreshments—even water was forbidden—during breaks in play, so when Holkar was fielding the drinks trolley returned much as it came. The only exception he would allow was for Denis Compton, for even C.K. did not expect an Englishman to go out unassisted in the tropical sun. So when Compton joined Holkar, at least one man could make proper use of the drinks break.

IV

As we have noticed, C.K. Nayudu spent the best years of his life battling against the whims of the princely patrons of Indian cricket. But even Nayudu himself would admit that at least three aristocratic families could play too. One was Patiala, whose crown prince, Yadavindra Singh, played under C.K. himself in a Test against Jardine's team. A big hitter like his townsman Navjot Sidhu, Yadavindra had scores of 24 and 60 in the match. Yadavindra's own father, Maharaja Bhupendra Singh, normally batted in full ceremonial dress, the glitter of the diamonds on his turban calculated no doubt to put the bowler off his length. A second, somewhat superior family of playing princes were the Pataudis, father and son, whose graceful batsmanship adorned cricket fields in four continents. But the claims of Patiala and Pataudi notwithstanding, the uncle and nephew from Nawanagar were surely the finest cricketing products of princely India.

The Jam Saheb (Ruler) of Nawanagar himself, K.S. Ranjitsinhji, played only 'social' cricket at home; to my knowledge he never appeared in a competitive match on Indian soil. His nephew K.S. Duleepsinhji was likewise a product of English cricket, but in his only first-class appearance in India he seems to have invented a shot whose parentage has more recently been claimed by their admirers for Mushtaq Mohammed and Ian Botham. Playing for the Hindus against the Parsis in the Quadrangular of 1928, Duleep scored 84 and 38. In the second innings, when the Hindus needed quick runs against a defensive field, Duleep crafted a shot which was described by his non-striker, L.P. Jai, as follows: 'Without changing the grip of the bat, he tried to hit the wide ball backwards towards the third-man with his bat turned and facing the wicket-keeper'. A perfect description of the 'reverse sweep', so Duleep must go down in cricket history as its inventor, even as his uncle is known as the inventor of the leg glance.

When the Ranji Trophy began in 1934, Duleep was not even thirty, but his cricket career had ended, owing to tuberculosis, some years before. However, after forming part of the Western India States Cricket Association (WISCA) in the first two years of the championship, Nawanagar, under the prodding of Duleep's brother Digvijaysinhji—the Jam Saheb after Ranji's death in 1931—entered a team for the competition. Astonishingly, in its first season this team won the Ranji Trophy. Its captain, not surprisingly, was a professional from the English country of Sussex which both Ranji and Duleep had led, A.F. Wensley. Although four princes also played under

Wensley in that year's final, only one, R.K. Ranvirsinhji, was heard of thereafter, when he was a late selection for the Australian tour of 1947. The side's wicket-keeper and opening batsman was Salim Durrani's father, Abdul Aziz, capped for India in an unofficial 'Test'. Nawanagar's batting in its debut season was consolidated by two Parsis, S.M.H. Colah and N.D. Marshall, both of whom accompanied the 1932 team to England. The team's fast bowler was S. Mubarak Ali, a player of international class whose career unfortunately overlapped with Mohammed Nissar's.

V

The two great cricketers of that Nawanagar side were the all-rounders Vinoo Mankad and Amar Singh. Both grew up in Jamnagar, Nawanagar's capital, and were the state's most precious gift to Indian cricket. Mankad, who at the age of nineteen scored 185 in the winning final against Bengal, was fashioned by A.F. Wensley as a slow left-arm bowler. His bowling has been treated in the chapter on Bombay; it remains for us to consider his batting here.

In a career studded with glittering deeds, Mankad's achievements in his *annus mirabilis*, 1952, stand out. In February and October of that year, he spun India to its first Test victories. In between, in the month of July, Mankad emerged from the Lancashire League to join the Indian team for the Second Test at Lord's. A vivid account of his batsmanship on that occasion comes from the pen of Alec Bedser, at the time England's leading bowler. Mankad, recalled Bedser, attacked the bowling from the first ball of the match,

taking unheard of liberties for a Test. His spirited on-slaught took the carefree attitude of Saturday afternoon

161

cricket into the stern atmosphere of the Tests . . . In the first half hour, when most Test openers are grimly concentrating on preserving their wickets, Mankad clouted Roly Jenkins for a huge six into the Mound Stand. When he had recovered, Roly, never at a loss for words, said: 'hey, what do you think this is—a Sunday benefit game?'

This was in the first innings. After bowling 73 overs when England batted, Mankad went in to open India's second innings late on the third day. He took up where he had left off, this time pulling Jenkins' first ball for six. He went on to score a magnificent 184 with scarcely a false stroke, in four and a half hours.

If his slow left-arm bowling was orthodoxy personified, Mankad's batting style, as befitting a son of Nawanagar, was very much his own. On the England tour of 1946, Mankad would invariably ask his opening partner Merchant as they walked out to bat: 'What cricket do you want me to play today, Vijay—English [i.e. orthodox] or Indian [i.e. unorthodox]?'

Himself the epitome of classical batsmanship, Vijay Merchant seemed to attract such mavericks, for Nawanagar's other great all-rounder, Amar Singh, was his closest friend in cricket, and they even named their sons for each other. Like Mankad, Amar Singh's bowling was orthodox; a master of swing and cut, he not unexpectedly thrived in English conditions. His batting was another matter altogether. As Cardus wrote after his dazzling half century in the Lord's Test of 1932, Amar 'upset Occidental logic' by his off-side hitting. He batted 'according to a secret of his own, [for] the blood in him tells him that reason, as the Occident knows it, is not the final truth in cricket'.

It is not generally known that Amar Singh's rise to

cricketing greatness owed something to Ranji's discerning eye. In a trial match for the 1932 tour of England, played at Delhi's beautiful **Roshanara Gardens**, Amar took none for plenty, although he did hit one six into the street, the ball striking a *tangawalla*. Ranji, who was watching, was impressed with the youngster's control and perseverance, and insisted his Nawanagar subject be selected for the tour. His advice was taken, and the rest is history.

Amar Singh died tragically of pneumonia at the age of thirty. Even while he lived, however, he was obsessed with death. Learie Constantine, who knew of this obsession, skilfully played upon it whenever his team, Nelson, met Amar Singh's side, Colne, in the Lancashire League. Learie was not above a little gamesmanship, and would invariably arrive for this particular match dressed in black. When the Indian all-rounder enquired about his dress, Learie, hoping to put him off his stride, would reply that he had just come from a funeral. This is, in its own way, a remarkable tribute to Amar Singh's cricketing genius.

In cricketing memory, Amar Singh's name will forever be paired with that of the Farrukhabad Express, Mohammed Nissar. There is a delightful story which illustrates the contrast between the brooding Amar Singh and the expansive Nissar. On the 1932 tour, Nissar came up against Frank Woolley, rated by C.K. Nayudu to be England's best batsman. The fast bowler told his teammates, '*Ek muh par doonga, dusra bhish karoonga*' (I'll bounce once at his face and then shatter his stumps). When Woolley hooked the first bouncer for six, Nissar muttered as he walked past mid-on to the top of his run, '*Ab dant tut jayega*' (Now I shall break his teeth). He sent down another bumper, which Woolley again hooked ferociously. Exclaimed an axasperated

Nissar : *'Baap re baap ye toh shaitan hai'* (Oh God! This fellow is a devil).*

It was altogether a rare occurrence for Nissar to be manhandled thus, for he was a formidable bowler. With Amar Singh he formed a partnership since unequalled in Indian cricket, despite the exertions of the Cricket Board and, more recently, of private sponsors convinced that fire must only be answered with fire. Indeed, the pair had England at 19 for 3 in the first hour of India's first Test match, and with back-up support must surely have won the match for their side.

VI

While Amar Singh relied on movement in the air and off the wicket, his elder brother Ramji, like Nissar, was a fast bowler pure and simple. With his forehead painted with red vermilion paste, Ramji cut a terrifying figure as he ran up to bowl for the Hindus in the Quadrangular. He was, however, past his prime when he played his only Test, against England at Bombay in 1933.

Although Ramji played for WISCA in the early years of the competition, he had retired by the time Nawanagar entered a team in the Ranji Trophy. It is, I believe, entirely legitimate to include him, as a son of Jamnagar, in an all-time Nawanagar XI. By the same token, we may include Ranji and Duleep as well.

But if our time frame can be stretched backwards, it can be stretched forward too. Thus, Nawanagar lost its political as well as cricketing identity in 1947, whereupon, with other former Rajput chiefdoms of northern Gujarat it formed the Saurashtra Cricket Association. Saurashtra scorecards of the nineteen-

* As told in K.V. Gopala Ratnam, 'Mohammed Nissar—Genuine Speed', *Indian Cricket, 1971.*

sixties have a distinctly old-world look about them, especially the ubiquity of the initials 'K.S.'. Standing for 'Kumar Shri', they signify, as they did for Ranji and Duleep, the bearer's status as a Rajput prince.

At least eight princes—all coached at the school where Ranji himself first learnt to play cricket, Rajkumar College, Rajkot—have appeared for Saurashtra in the Ranji Trophy. One of them was the present Jam Saheb, known in his playing days simply as K.S. Shatushalyasinhji. Another was K.S. Chatrapalsinhji, the Air India officer whose brainchild the 1989 Nehru Cup was. But the finest cricketer of the lot was their close kinsman, K.S. Indrajitsinhji. Growing up in Jamnagar, Indrajit was both educated and coached at the palace. As a wicket-keeper-batsman, Indrajit had fierce competition for the Test team; for as Sujit Mukherjee observed, he had to outbat Kunderan and outkeep Engineer if he was to wear India colours. He did so successfully one season, 1964, keeping immaculately and playing a death or glory innings in the one Test India won. Appropriately, given his lineage, it was against Australia, the country against which Ranji and Duleep had played their own finest innings.

VII

With Aziz available, Indrajit can play as a batsman. Our all-time Nawanagar XI can then read:

1. V. Mankad
2. K.S. Indrajitsinhji
3. K.S. Ranjitsinhji (captain)
4. K.S. Duleepsinhji
5. N.D. Marshall
6. S.M.H. Colah

7. L. Amar Singh
8. A.F. Wensley
9. Abdul Aziz (wicket-keeper)
10. L. Ramji
11. S. Mubarak Ali

VIII

Perhaps the title of this chapter was somewhat premature. For India's most promising spinner, Narendra Hirwani, moved to Indore as a young boy. Since then, he has been coached by Sanjay Jagdale, the son of C.K.'s own colleague M.M. And as I write, Duleep's grandnephew Ajay Jadeja (whose father served four terms as Member of Parliament from Jamnagar) is, as an attacking opening batsman, on the margins of the Indian Test side. An outstandingly successful member of the Indian under-nineteen team, Jadeja has already served in the senior national team for a one day tournament. Nawanagar and Holkar may have long since fallen down the trapdoor history, but the traditions of C.K. and Ranji live on.

CHAPTER NINE

Remainders

*H*eard melodies are sweet, but those unheard are sweeter. In writing this book, I have been continually reminded of this line from Keats that A.A. Thomson was fond of quoting. For, in the beginning, I never thought that I would come to place cricketers whom I had never seen alongside my boyhood heroes in Bangalore. But in the end, I cannot honestly claim that G.R. Viswanath was a more elegant batsman than Vijay Hazare, or Erapalli Prasanna a more artful off-spinner than Ghulam Ahmed.

A second, equally important revelation has been the hold on the folk imagination of 'local' heroes who may never have played for India. In the collective memory of the Calcutta Maidan, Kartik Bose, who did not play a Test, will always be regarded as highly as his fellow opener Pankaj Roy, who played long and successfully in the international arena. Likewise, the Madras cricket lover has as much place for A.G. Ram Singh, uncapped in an official 'Test', as he does for Srinivas Venkataraghavan, who represented India with honour in five countries.

Now, as a final celebration of the regional cultures of Indian cricket, I shall choose an all-time eleven from the ten cities and states whose folk histories I have retold. There are only two boundary conditions: each team shall send a 'local' hero whose genius was never recognized by the Indian Test selectors, and Bombay will be allowed the privilege of sending two players to our selection.

Bengal must, of course, nominate a representative from its martial tradition of seam bowling. D.S. Mukherjee and Barun Barman are two equally strong contenders here. But as Bengalis are far more sensitive to history than, for example, the Punjabis, we may settle for Kamal Bhattacharjee, respected coach and playing member of that very European Ranji Trophy winning side of 1938-9.

By the same token, Bombay's choices must be a left-arm spinner and a batsman respectively. Given our condition that no one must have played an official Test, there can be only one choice as left-arm spinner—Padmakar Shivalkar. However, the line of great Bombay batsmen who never played for India is almost as long as the line of those who did. Among the Parsis, one cannot easily overlook the claims of that big-hitting left-hander, D.R. 'Dadi' Havewalla, or of Rusi Cooper, a strokemaker as elegant as his cousin and namesake, Rusi Modi. Cultured Maratha strokeplayers of a later vintage include the two Vijays, Bhonsle and Paranjype. My own fancy, however, is for that Pocket Hercules among opening batsmen, Sudhakar Adhikari. Desperately unlucky not to have been chosen for India in the nineteen-sixties, Adhikari had a range of strokes fully the equal of Gavaskar's, though he lived far more dangerously off the field, ending up in a London jail on charges of drug smuggling.

From Delhi, we must choose a Punjabi exile, preferably a University product. The man who meets these twin criteria best is Akash Lal of Hindu College, also member of a famous cricketing family. Akash's father, Muni Lal, opened the batting for Northern India in the Ranji Trophy, produced half a dozen volumes of a pioneering cricket annual, 'Crickinia', served as Indian High Commissioner to Fiji, and wrote biographies of several Mughal emperors to boot. For Muni's younger brother, Jagdish Lal, variety was to be found on the cricket field itself; he opened the batting for as many as eight teams in the Ranji Trophy. Jagdish's own son, Arun Lal, was the first member of the family to be capped for India, but Arun would readily admit that cousin Akash was by far the better strokeplayer.

Hyderabad presents a ticklish problem, as it is difficult to find a candidate from one of the city's two cricketing cultures. We may settle then for E.B. Aibara, whose coaching clinics have always been open to nawab and commoner alike.

Mysore's nominee, B. Frank, perfectly embodies the gaiety of the state's cricketing ethos. Benjamin Frank enjoyed the game as much as did B.S. Chandrasekhar, while his integrity matched that of Vishy himself.

Tamil Nadu must send a member of its turbaned first family. None better than the patriarch, Amritsar Gurugobind Ram Singh. Ram would also be captain of our team, in which capacity he would, as a good Dravidian nationalist, strictly prohibit the use of Hindi on the field—only Tamil and English allowed here.

Baroda and Rajasthan shall, of course, send a prince apiece. The claims of H.H. Baroda and H.H. Mewar are formidable indeed. But on purely cricketing grounds, we must choose Jackie Baroda's younger brother, Sangram Gaekwad, and Udaipur's fellow Sisodia ruler, Suryaveer Singh of Banswara.

In contrast, Nawanagar and Holkar will nominate commoners. From the land of Amar Singh and Ramji, we may choose a fast bowler, S. Mubarak Ali, while C.K. Nayudu would no doubt have recommended J.N. Bhaya, a fielder to match the Old Man in his prime.

This then is the last eleven we shall choose. A team of 'local heroes', but Heroes nevertheless.

1. S.G. Adhikari (Bombay)
2. S.P. Gaekwad (Baroda)
3. Akash Lal (Delhi)
4. E.B. Aibara (Hyderabad)
5. B. Frank (Karnataka)
6. A.G. Ram Singh (Tamil Nadu: captain)
7. Suryaveer Singh (Rajasthan: wicket-keeper)
8. J.N. Bhaya (Holkar)
9. K. Bhattacharjee (Bengal)
10. S. Mubarak Ali (Nawanagar)
11. P. Shivalkar (Bombay)

Index

◈❧◈

Qasim, I., 95

Rae, A., 22, 113
Raghunath, B., 109
Rai, G., 66
Rajagopal, K.R., 108, 113
Raj Singh, 142, 151, 152
Raju, V., 81
Ram, N., 130
Ramadhin, S., 157
Raman, W.V., 113
Ramaswami, C., 2–5, 106, 112, 121–2, 123, 129
Ramchand, G.S., 20, 31, 42, 141, 152
Ramdev, C.J., 107
Ramesh, P., 122
Ramji, L., 164, 165, 169
Ramnarayan, V., 80
Ram Singh, A.G., 5, 105, 123–4, 126–7, 129, 167, 169, 170
Randall, D.W., 92
Rangachari, C.R., 112–3, 122n, 130
Rangnekar, K.M., 31, 157, 158
Ranjitsinhji, K.S., 9, 35, 41, 66, 73, 124–5n, 148, 153, 160, 162, 164, 165
Ranvirsinhji, R.K., 160–1
Reddy, B., 129, 130
Reddy, N.S.K., 71
Rege, M.D., 46, 97, 99
Rhodes, W., 30, 44, 45, 64, 107, 114, 149
Richards, I.V.A., 6, 51, 92, 114
Ridgway, F., 139
Roberts, A.M.E., 38, 119, 137
Robertson, J.D., 44
Robinson, E., 34
Roy, Ambar, 13, 14, 17, 18, 28
Roy, Amitava, 14, 22
Roy, Pankaj, 12, 13, 17–9, 26, 27, 28, 167

Roy, Pronob, 17
Rungta, K.M., 142, 147
Ryder, J.S., 122, 124

Sadiq Mahommed, 102
Saleem, S., 78
Sarangapani, A.K., 113
Sardesai, D.N., 17, 30, 31, 40, 50, 100
Sarkar, D., 14, 20, 60
Sarwate, C.T., 157, 158
Satwender Singh, A.G., 126
Saxena, R., 66, 67
Sen, P., 12, 13, 16, 28, 45, 48
Seshachar, K., 128
Shah, R., 141
Shaktawat, G.S., 99
Sharma, C., 54
Sharma, P., 142–3, 147
Sharma, Y., 57
Shatrushalyasinhji, K.S., 165
Shinde, S.G., 46, 50, 135, 152
Shivalkar, P., 20, 30, 46, 50, 78, 97, 100, 120, 168, 170
Shivram, P., 36
Shodhan, D.H., 90, 124–5n, 139, 140
Shukla, R., 63, 66
Sidhu, N.S., 58, 159
Simpson, R.B., 38
Sivaramakrishnan, L., 20, 43, 120
Sivaramakrishnan, V., 121
Smith, M.J.K., 88
Sobers, G.S., 38, 42, 43, 84, 85, 89, 105, 112, 119, 143, 144
Sohoni, S.W., 2, 152
Solkar, E.D., 8, 34–9, 42, 50, 60, 79, 99, 100, 114, 120
Sood, M.M., 52, 62, 66, 67
Srikkanth, K., 63, 76, 104, 106, 113, 116–9, 129
Srinivasan, M.O., 128–9

Index

Srinivasan, T.E. 113
Stollmeyer, J.B., 44, 113
Subrahmanyam, V., 40, 85, 106, 108
Sudhakar Rao, 98–9, 106, 108, 109
Sunderam, G.R., 31, 142, 147
Sunderam, V., 88
Surendranath, 139
Surti, R.F., 32, 38
Suryanarayana, M., 122
Suryaveer Singh, 142, 147, 169, 170
Sutcliffe, H., 30, 34, 70
Swaranjit Singh, 19

Tallon, D., 128
Tamhane, N.S., 48, 50
Tarapore, K.K., 46
Tate, F., 136
Tate, M.W., 137
Tendulkar, S., 30, 31, 34
Tennyson, L., 124
Thomson, J., 56, 61
Tribe, G., 17, 105, 156
Trueman, F.S., 18, 40, 44, 63, 134
Trumble, H., 149
Trumper, V.T., 133

Umrigar, P.R., 7, 30, 32, 34, 40, 41, 47, 50, 72
Underwood, D.L., 95, 144

Vajifdar, H., 104
Valson, S., 52
Vengsarkar, D.B., 7, 31, 33, 40, 41, 50, 141

Venkataraghavan, S., 20, 23, 36, 38, 46, 51, 79, 113–6, 118, 119, 120, 130, 167
Venkataramunujulu, M., 121, 122
Venkatesh, R., 75
Verity, H., 30, 45, 64
Vijaykrishna, B., 86, 109
Vijaykumar, V.S., 97, 104, 109
Viswanath, G.R., 7–8, 16, 17, 34, 46, 85, 88, 89–98, 100, 101, 106, 108, 109, 132, 133, 147, 155, 167, 169
Viswanath, P.S., 105, 106
Viswanath, S., 104
Vithal, P., 35–6

Wadekar, A.L., 11, 17, 18, 33, 37, 38, 40, 41, 47, 50, 73, 75, 79, 83, 90, 98–100, 144
Wainwright, E., 41
Walcott, C.L., 113
Wardle, J.H., 30
Waugh, S., 133
Weekes, E.D., 14, 104, 113
Wensley, A.F., 36, 126, 160, 161, 165
Willis, R.G.D., 92, 117
Wood, B., 64
Woolley, F.E., 121, 163
Worrell, F.M.M., 5, 14, 16, 44, 113

Yadav, N.S., 43, 80–1, 82
Yajuvendra Singh, 156
Yuvraj of Patiala, 123, 159

Zaheer Abbas, 102–3

177